I0818867

FIFA

THE ILLUSTRATED HISTORy OF

SOCCER WORLD CUP

1930 – 2026

THE ILLUSTRATED HISTORY OF

SOCCER WORLD CUP

1930–2026

-AczeL-

DEFENDING CHAMPIONS ARGENTINA

CONTENTS

1930 URUGUAY

URUGUAY (LEFT) AND ARGENTINA ARE LED TO THE FIELD BY THEIR CAPTAINS JOSE NASAZZI AND MANUEL FERREIRA

1930 URUGUAY

Seized weapons, snow flurries and a boat to escape! The first Soccer World Cup was an adventure, from the modern point of view. Only 13 teams participated in the tournament in Uruguay (from July 13 to July 30). The European players, who had a mentality inspired by the Olympic spirit, looked down on South American players, who were playing professionally for money for the first time.

The national soccer team of Uruguay displayed the highest level of soccer in the Olympic Games in 1924 and 1928, and won gold medals on both occasions. These two victories and the 100th anniversary of the country were the two main reasons to choose Montevideo, the capital city of Uruguay, to host the first World Cup.FIFA (Federation Internationale de Football Association) was founded in 1904. Jules Rimet, President of FIFA from 1921 to 1954, and Enrique Buero, a wealthy Uruguayan owner of a cattle ranch, developed ideas for a world tournament in 1924.

THE CUP, JULES RIMET, THREE REFEREES AND THREE EUROPEAN TEAMS TRAVELLED ABOARD THE S.S. CONTE VERDE. THE BRAZILIAN TEAM JOINED THEM IN RIO DE JANEIRO

FIFA PRESIDENT JULES RIMET (LEFT) AND DR. PAUL JUDE, PRESIDENT OF URUGUAYAN FOOTBALL ASSOCIATION ARE ADMIRING THE CUP

Seven teams from Latin America, apart from the host, attended the event. They were Argentina, the South American Champion, Bolivia, Peru, Chile, Brazil, Paraguay and Mexico. United States of America represented the North of America. From Europe, France, Belgium, Romania and Yugoslavia crossed the Atlantic Ocean by sea and arrived after a two-week voyage. Many other teams did not attend due to the expensive costs and the length of the journey. The German Football Association justified its absence with the same arguments, but probably the players preferred not to play against their former war enemies. The championship in Uruguay was the only World Cup in which the teams joined the competition without qualifications. The draws took place in Montevideo. The first group had four teams while the rest were divided into three groups of three teams each. 4,444 enthusiastic spectators witnessed the opening match. France faced Mexico cn July 13, at 3 pm in Pocitos Stadium. It was a snowy winter, uncommon in the area,

THE WORLD CUP MADE OF PURE GOLD, WITH THE NAME OF JULES RIMET ON IT

ESTADIO CENTENARIO

ANDRADE, THE EXCEPTIONAL URUGUAYAN PLAYER

but no cold weather could freeze so much passion. After 19 minutes of the game, Lucien Laurent, the 1.60 m tall forward player from France, scored the first goal in the World Cup history. “All I did was to score a goal, never imagined how important it would be in the future,” said Laurent decades later. France defeated Mexico 4-1.

The favorite teams were Argentina and Uruguay, who topped their groups as expected. In semifinals, both teams were clearly superior: Argentina defeated the United States and Uruguay won against Yugoslavia. Both games finished 6-1.

Almost 80,000 attended the final match on July 30. They were thoroughly searched to avoid any violence. Nearly 1,600 weapons were confiscated at the stadium. The referee, John Langenus from Antwerp, 1.90 m tall, properly dressed in a suit and tie requested a boat ready at the harbour, in case he needed to make a quick escape. Uruguay, with a final score of 4-2 became the first ever champion of the World Cup. The next day was declared a national holiday.

LUCIEN LAURENT FROM FRANCE EARNED A PLACE IN HISTORY BY SCORING THE FIRST GOAL IN A WORLD CUP...

1ST WORLD CUP GOAL

...AND THIS WAS HOW IT HAPPENED

13TH JULY, 1930. ESTADIO POCITOS 19TH MINUTE

1930 WORLD CHAMPIONS: URUGUAY. TOP: ERNESTO "MATUCHO" FÍGOLI (MASSEUR), Á_VARO GESTIDO, JOSÉ NASAZZI, ENRIQUE BALLSTEROS, ERNESTO MASCHERONI, JOSÉ ANDRADE, LORENZO FERNÁNDEZ BOTTOM: PABLO DORADO, HÉCTOR SCARONE, HÉCTOR CASTRO, PEDRO CEA, SANTOS IRIARTE

ALBERTO SUPICCI, THE URUGUAYAN COACH GAVE HIS PLAYERS FREEDOM OF ACTION

THE FINAL 30TH JULY, 1930

URUGUAY 4:2 ARGENTINA

ESTADIO CENTENARIO, MONTEVIDEO, URUGUAY
ATTENDANCE: 80,000
REFEREE: JOHN LANGENUS (BELGIUM)

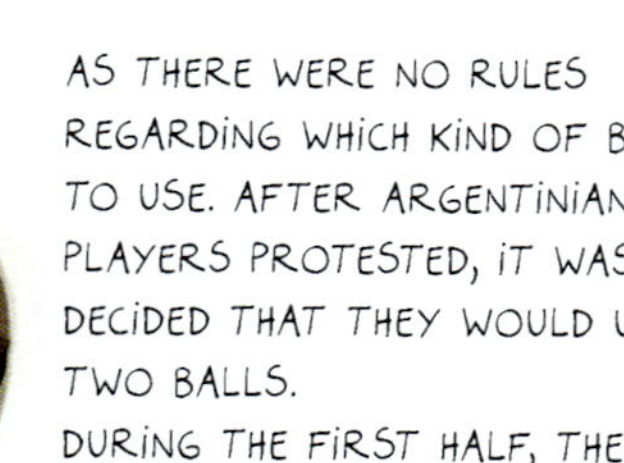

AS THERE WERE NO RULES REGARDING WHICH KIND OF BALL TO USE. AFTER ARGENTINIAN PLAYERS PROTESTED, IT WAS DECIDED THAT THEY WOULD USE TWO BALLS.
DURING THE FIRST HALF, THE ARGENTINIAN BALL WAS USED AND IN THE SECOND HALF THE URUGUAYAN ONE

1:0
DORADO NUTMEGS BOTASSO
12TH MINUTE
1:1
PEUCELLE DRAWS
20TH MINUTE
1:2
STÁBILE
37TH MINUTE
2:2
CEA SCORES WITH A SHORT SHOT
57TH MINUTE
3:2
SANTOS IRIARTE FROM 27 METRES AWAY
68TH MINUTE
4:2
CASTRO HEADS HOME
89TH MINUTE
URUGUAY WORLD CHAMPION!
ACZEL

1930 IN OVERVIEW

GROUP 1

DATE	TEAM	R	TEAM
13.07.	FRANCE	4:1	MEXICO
15.07.	ARGENTINA	1:0	FRANCE
16.07.	CHILE	3:0	MEXICO
19.07.	CHILE	1:0	FRANCE
19.07.	ARGENTINA	6:3	MEXICO
22.07.	ARGENTINA	3:1	CHILE

GROUP 2

DATE	TEAM	R	TEAM
14.07.	YUGOSLAVIA	2:1	BRAZIL
17.07.	YUGOSLAVIA	4:0	BOLIVIA
20.07.	BRAZIL	4:0	BOLIVIA

GROUP 3

DATE	TEAM	R	TEAM
14.07.	ROMANIA	3:1	PERU
18.07.	URUGUAY	1:0	PERU
21.07	URUGUAY	4:0	ROMANIA

GROUP 4

DATE	TEAM	R	TEAM
13.07.	USA	3:0	BELGIUM
17.07.	USA	3:0	PARAGUAY
20.07.	PARAGUAY	1:0	BELGIUM

SEMIFINALS

DATE	TEAM	R	TEAM
26.07.	ARGENTINA	6:1	USA
26.07.	URUGUAY	6:1	YUGOSLAVIA

FINAL

DATE	TEAM	R	TEAM
30.07.	URUGUAY	4:2	ARGENTINA

TICKET 1930

HANDSHAKE BEFORE THE FIRST FINAL OF WORLD CUP HISTORY

THE SHOES WERE RUSTIC, HARD AND UNCOMFORTABLE

EACH PLAYER RECEIVED A MEDAL AS SOUVENIR

CHAMPION: URUGUAY

QUALIFIED TEAMS
13 (FROM 13 CANDIDATES)

PERIOD
13TH JULY, 1930–30TH JULY, 1930

ATTENDANCE
590,549 (Ø: 32,808 PER MATCH)

PLAYERS IN FIELD

189

GOALS
70 (Ø: 3.89 PER MATCH)

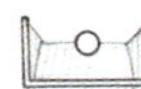

OWN GOALS
1

FASTEST GOAL
50 SECONDS: DEU
(ROMANIA–PERU)

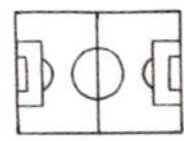

MATCHES
18

MOST DANGEROUS TEAM
ARGENTINA: 18 GOALS
IN 5 MATCHES

TOP SCORERS
8 GOALS: STÁBILE (ARGENTINA)
5 GOALS: CEA (URUGUAY)
4 GOALS: PATENAUDE (USA)

EXPULSIONS
1 (Ø: 0.06 PER MATCH)

BEST PLAYER TOP 3
1. JOSÉ LEANDRO ANDRADE (URUGUAY)
2. GUILLERMO STÁBILE (ARGENTINA)
3. JOSÉ PEDRO CEA (URUGUAY)

BEST GOALKEEPER
ENRIQUE BALLSTERO (URUGUAY)

3 OR MORE GOALS IN ONE MATCH
3 GOALS: STÁBILE (ARGENTINA–MEXICO)
PATENAUDE (USA–PARAGUAY)
CEA (URUGUAY–YUGOSLAVIA)

PENALTIES
4: 1 SCORED, 3 MISSED/SAVED

DREAM TEAM 1930

1934 ITALY

ITALY STRUGGLES AND DEFEATS CZECHOSLOVAKIA DURING EXTRA-TIME

1934 ITALY

A dictator abuses sports as political scenery; first hat-trick in World Cup history, Germany, a great force enters the World Cup for the first time along with an unbeatable Austria! Here are all the milestones of the second edition of the World Cup that took place in Italy from May 27 to June 10.

32 National Teams played qualification matches. Only 16 of them would participate in the World Cup. Among them, Egypt was the first African country to participate. Uruguay, the last champion, was upset that Italy had not come to their party in 1930. They decided not to attend as a response.

The leader Benito Mussolini had four stadiums built by means of the national treasury and took advantage of the sport for fascist propaganda. The matches were played by K.O. system. Brazil and Argentina had to go back home after the preliminary round. Germany crushed Belgium 5-2; thanks to the three goals scored by Edmund "Ed" Conen in the 66th, 70th and 87th minutes of the match, thus scoring the first hat-trick in World Cup history.

Austria played against Germany with the blue shirts of Napoli, as both teams traditionally wore black and white kits, and won 3-2. In quarter-finals Spain and Italy faced one another, a match that the Azzurri should have won, ended in a draw 1-1 after extra time. A replay match was played the following day, in which plenty of violence and a controversial performance of the referee in favor of the Italian team was seen. (Penalties were introduced in a later edition of the World Cups.) The host won 1-0.

In another quarter-final, Austria defeated Hungary (2-1). Austrian players were favorites but Italy ended their winning streak by defeating them (1-0). During the final match on June 10th in Rome, Italy was again favored by the referee, who did not punish the Azzurri's faults. However, its opponent Czechoslovakia was still leading the match, until the moment in which Giuseppe Meazza passed the ball to striker Angelo Schiavo who smashed the winning shot into the goal, and Italy became champions of the World Cup for the first time.

GIUSEPPE MEAZZA, THE LEGENDARY CENTRE FORWARD, WAS SO BELOVED THAT THEY NAMED AC MILAN'S STADIUM AFTER HIM

1934 WORLD CHAMPIONS: ITALY.
TOP: GIAMPIERO COMBI, LUISITO MONTI, ATTILIO FERRARIS, LUIGI ALLMANDI, ENRICO GUAITA, GIOVANNI FERRARI. BOTTOM: ANGELO SCHIAVIO, GIUSEPPE MEAZZA, ERALDO MONZEGLIO, LUIGI BERTOLINI, RAIMONDO ORSI

A DEFINING GOAL SCORED BY MEAZZA FOR ITALY IN THE REPLAY MATCH AGAINST SPAIN

OLDRICH NEJEDLÝ FROM CZECHOSLOVAKIA; TOP SCORER WITH FIVE GOALS

ALMOST EMPTY STADIUMS. THE FANS PREFFERRED LOCAL CHAMPIONSHIP MATCHES...

IT WAS THE WORLD CUP OF THE GOALKEEPERS. RICARDO ZAMORA, FROM SPAIN ONE OF THE CELEBRITIES OF THOSE TIMES

THE FINAL

10TH JUNE, 1934

ITALY 2:1 CZECHOSLOVAKIA (EXTRA-TIME)
STADIO NAZIONALE DEL PNF, ROME
ATTENDANCE: 55,000
REFEREE: IVAN EKLIND (SWEDEN)

ITALIAN COACH VITTORIO POZZO BECAME FAMOUS FOR HIS PERFECT ARRANGEMENTS

THE ONLY FINAL MATCH IN WHICH BOTH GOALKEEPERS WERE CAPTAINS OF THEIR TEAMS

55TH MINUTE
PUC IS DENIED A PENALTY...

...AND THEN HE IS CARRIED OFF INJURED

0:1
PUC RETURNS AND SCORES
76TH MINUTE

1:1
ORSI EQUALISES
81ST MINUTE

EXTRA-TIME

SCHIAVIO RECEIVES A PASS FROM MEAZZA AND...
95TH MINUTE

2 : 1
...GOAL!!!
ITALY WORLD CHAMPION!!!

1934 IN OVERVIEW

FIRST ROUND

DATE	TEAM	R	TEAM
27.05.	SWEDEN	3:2	ARGENTINA
27.05.	AUSTRIA	3:2	FRANCE
27.05.	GERMANY	5:2	BELGIUM
27.05.	SPAIN	3:1	BRAZIL
27.05.	HUNGARY	4:2	EGYPT
27.05.	SWITZERLAND	3:2	NETHERLANDS
27.05.	ITALY	7:1	USA
27.05.	CZECHOSLOVAKIA	2:1	ROMANIA

SEMIFINALS

DATE	TEAM	R	TEAM
03.06.	ITALY	1:0	AUSTRIA
03.06.	CZECHOSL.	3:1	GERMANY

3RD PLACE

DATE	TEAM	R	TEAM
07.06.	GERMANY	3:2	AUSTRIA

QUARTER-FINALS

DATE	TEAM	R	TEAM
31.05.	CZECHOSL.	3:2	SWITZERLAND
31.05.	GERMANY	2:1	SWEDEN
31.05.	ITALY	1:1	SPAIN
31.05.	AUSTRIA	2:1	HUNGARY
*31.05.	ITALY	1:1	SPAIN

* 01.06. REPLAY MATCH: 1:0

FINAL

DATE	TEAM	R	TEAM
10.06.	ITALY	2:1	CZECHOSL.

TICKET
1934

CHAMPION: ITALY

"OUR SUCCESS IS A REWARD FOR HARD WORK, MORAL STEADFASTNESS, A SPIRIT OF SELF-SACRIFICE, AND THE UNSHAKEABLE DESIRE OF A GROUP OF MEN," ITALY COACH VITTORIO POZZO SAID

QUALIFIED TEAMS
16 (FROM 32 CANDIDATES)

PERIOD
27TH MAY, 1934–10TH JUNE, 1934

ATTENDANCE
363,000 (Ø: 21,353 PER MATCH)

PLAYERS IN FIELD
208

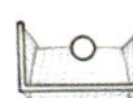

GOALS
70 (Ø: 4.12 PER MATCH)

OWN GOALS
0

FASTEST GOAL
25 SECONDS: LEHNER
(GERMANY–AUSTRIA)

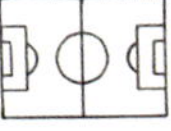

MATCHES
17

MOST DANGEROUS TEAM
ITALY: 12 GOALS IN 5 MATCHES

TOP SCORERS
5 GOALS: NEJEDLÝ
(CZECHOSLOVAKIA)
4 GOALS: SCHIAVIO (ITALY)
CONEN (GERMANY)

EXPULSIONS
1 (Ø: 0.06 PER MATCH)

BEST PLAYER TOP 3
1. GIUSEPPE MEAZZA (ITALY)
2. OLDICH NEJEDLÝ (CZECHOSLOVAKIA)
3. ANGELO SCHIAVIO (ITALY)

BEST GOALKEEPER
RICARDO ZAMORA (SPAIN)

3 OR MORE GOALS IN A MATCH
3 GOALS: SCHIAVIO (ITALY–USA)
CONEN (GERMANY–BELGIUM)
NEJEDLÝ (CZECHOSLOVAKIA–GERMANY)

PENALTIES
4: 3 SCORED, 1 MISSED

DREAM TEAM 1934

1938 FRANCE

1938 WORLD CUP WAS ORGANISED IN ITS SPIRITUAL HOME, PARIS

1938 FRANCE

The third World Cup was held in France, from June 4 to 19, immersed in a somber political climate prior to the Second World War, having been chosen as host over Argentina two years earlier.

The German coach, Sepp Herberger, had to set up a completely new team in only ten weeks. Due to the annexation of Austria by the Nazis that same year, officials demanded the creation of a 'Greater Germany' team, which had to include both German and Austrian players. 16 teams qualified for the tournament, including the Dutch East Indies (now Indonesia) and Cuba, which was the only time they participated. South American teams Argentina and Uruguay were the great absentees, as they believed that Argentina deserved to host the Cup. Spain missed the Cup, as it was enveloped in a civil war.

Germany was beaten by Switzerland in the first round. Some German players, who used the fascist salute, were booed by the audience.

During the match between Brazil and Poland, that ended 6-5 for Brazil, the fans enjoyed the play of Leônidas da Silva, called the 'black diamond'. He played barefoot for a while and scored three times for Brazil. In the brutal quarter-finals, Czech goalkeeper, František Plánička, became a hero by continuing to play despite a broken arm, although he could not prevent a 2-1 defeat. Brazil seemed the clear favorite, but in the final stretch of the tournament they left the way open for the Italians. In the semifinals, they were eliminated, perhaps because coach Adhemar Pimenta decided to replace Leônidas da Silva. After the deserved result 2-1, the Azzurri faced Hungary in the final. Once again, the great Giuseppe Meazza led the Italian team, which won 4-2 to be crowned World Champion for the second consecutive time.

YVES, JULES RIMET GRANDSON, MAKES THE DRAW, AS HIS PROUD GRANDFATHER HOLDS THE JAR

IN 1938 BRAZIL WAS THE ONLY SOUTH AMERICAN COUNTRY THAT AGREED TO PARTICIPATE

THE GREAT FRANTIŠEK PLÁNIČKA, THE CZECH GOALKEEPER, CONTINUED TO PLAY WITH A BROKEN ARM!

COLAUSSI'S GOAL AT THE QUARTER-FINAL AGAINST FRANCE. DI LORTO STRUGGLES BUT IS NOT ENOUGH. THE ITALIAN TEAM PLAYS WITH BLACK SHIRTS, 'THE COLOR OF FASCISM'

THE NAZI SALUTE OF THE GERMAN TEAM WAS DISAPPROVED IN FRANCE

1938 WORLD CHAMPIONS: ITALY. TOP: BURLANDO (CO-TRAINER), AMEDEO BIAVATI, GIORGIO VACCARO (FIGC PRESIDENT), VITTORIO POZZO (COACH), ANGELI (MASSEUR) SILVIO PIOLA, GIOVANNI FERRARI, GINO COLAUSSI. BOTTOM: UGO LOCATELLI, GIUSEPPE MEAZZA ALFREDO FONI, PIETRO SERANTONI (LYING), ALDO OLIVIERI, PIETRO RAVA, MICHELE ANDREOLO

GIUSEPPE MEAZZA WON HIS SECOND WORLD CUP IN 1938...

...AS DID VICTORIO POZZO, THE GREAT ITALIAN COACH

THE FINAL

19TH JUNE, 1938

ITALY 4:2 HUNGARY

STADE OLYMPIQUE DE COLOMBES, PARIS

ATTENDANCE: 60,000

REFEREE: GEORGES CAPDEVILLE (FRANCE)

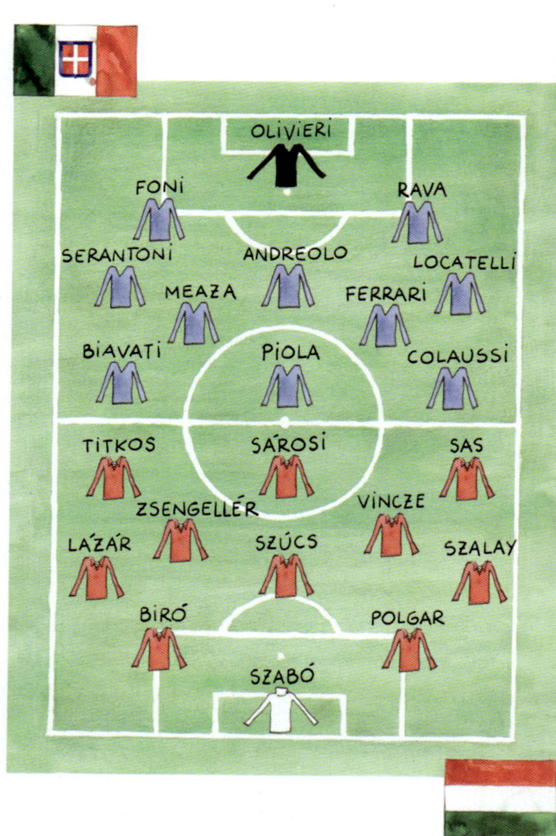

COUPE DU MONDE 1938

6TH MINUTE
1:0
PASS FROM PIOLA, COLAUSSI SCORES

7TH MINUTE
1:1
TITKOS EQUALISES

2:1
PIOLA. UNSTOPPABLE
16TH MINUTE

3:1
COLAUSSI SCORES BRILLIANTLY
35TH MINUTE

3:2
SAROSI SCORES FOR HUNGARY
70TH MINUTE

4:2
PIOLA DEFINES THE MATCH
82ND MINUTE

ITALY WORLD CHAMPION
HONGRIE 2
ITALIE 4

1938 IN OVERVIEW

FIRST ROUND

DATE	TEAM	R	TEAM
04.06.	SWITZERLAND	1:1	GERMANY
05.06.	HUNGARY	6:0	DUTCH EAST INDIES
05.06.	FRANCE	3:1	BELGIUM
05.06.	CUBA	3:3	ROMANIA
05.06.	ITALY	2:1	NORWAY
05.06.	BRAZIL	6:5	POLAND
05.06.	CZECHOSLOVAKIA	3:0	NETHERLANDS
*09.06.	CUBA	2:1	ROMANIA
*09.06.	SWITZERLAND	4:2	GERMANY

* REPLAY MATCH

QUARTER-FINALS

DATE	TEAM	R	TEAM
12.06.	BRAZIL	1:1	CZECHOSL.
12.06.	HUNGARY	2:0	SWITZERLAND
12.06.	SWEDEN	8:0	CUBA
12.06.	ITALY	3:1	FRANCE
*14.06.	BRAZIL	2:1	CZECHOSL.

* REPLAY MATCH

SEMIFINALS

DATE	TEAM	R	TEAM
16.06.	HUNGARY	5:1	SWEDEN
16.06.	ITALY	2:1	BRAZIL

3RD PLACE

DATE	TEAM	R	TEAM
19.06.	BRAZIL	4:2	SWEDEN

FINAL

DATE	TEAM	R	TEAM
19.06.	ITALY	4:2	HUNGARY

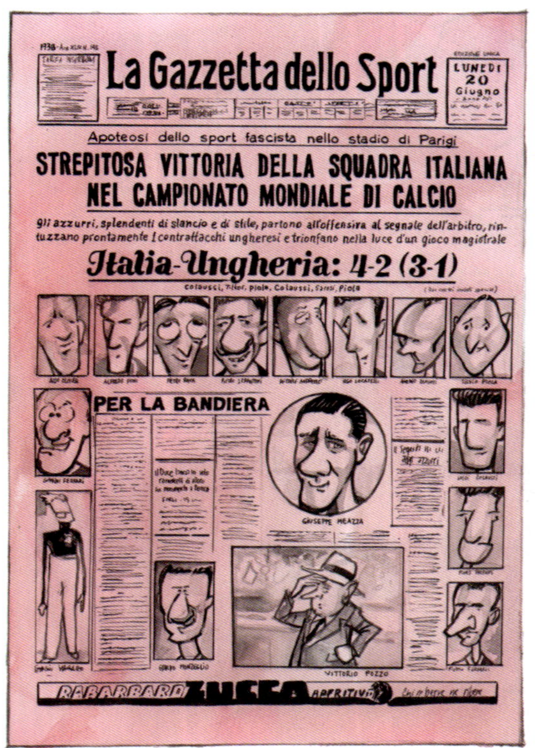

La Gazzetta dello Sport

LUNEDI 20 Giugno

Apoteosi dello sport fascista nello stadio di Parigi

STREPITOSA VITTORIA DELLA SQUADRA ITALIANA NEL CAMPIONATO MONDIALE DI CALCIO

gli azzurri, splendenti di slancio e di stile, partono all'offensiva al segnale dell'arbitro, rintuzzano prontamente i contrattacchi ungheresi e trionfano nella luce d'un gioco magistrale

Italia-Ungheria: 4-2 (3-1)

Colaussi, Titkos, Piola, Colaussi, Sarosi, Piola

PER LA BANDIERA

GIUSEPPE MEAZZA

VITTORIO POZZO

RABARBARO ZUCCA APERITIVO

CHAMPION: ITALY

TICKET 1938

FRONT PAGE OF ITALIAN NEWSPAPER 'LA GAZZETA DELLO SPORT' AFTER THE GREAT VICTORY IN PARIS

QUALIFIED TEAMS
15 (FROM 36 CANDIDATES)

PERIOD
04 JUNE 1938–19 JUNE 1938

ATTENDANCE
375,700 (Ø: 20,872 PER MATCH)

PLAYERS IN FIELD

211

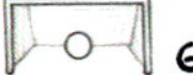

GOALS
84 (Ø: 4.67 PER MATCH)

OWN GOALS
2

FASTEST GOAL

35 SECONDS: ARNE NYBERG
(SWEDEN–HUNGARY)

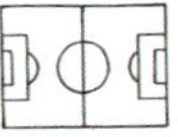

MATCHES
18

MOST DANGEROUS TEAM
HUNGARY: 15 GOALS IN 4 MATCHES

TOP SCORERS
8 GOALS: LEÔNIDAS (BRAZIL)
6 GOALS: ZSENGELLÉR (HUNGARY)
5 GOALS: PIOLA (ITALY), SAROSI (HUNGARY)

EXPULSIONS
4 (Ø: 0.22 PER MATCH)

BEST PLAYER TOP 3
1. SILVIO PIOLA (ITALY)
2. LEÔNIDAS (BRAZIL)
3. GIUSEPPE MEAZZA (ITALY)

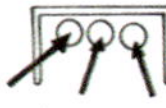

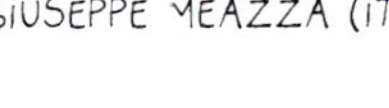

BEST GOALKEEPER
FRANTISEK PLÁNIČKA
(CZECHOSLOVAKIA)

3 OR MORE GOALS IN A MATCH
4 GOALS: LEÔNIDAS (BRAZIL–POLAND)
WILLIMOWSKI (POLAND–BRAZIL)
3 GOALS: WETTERSTRÖM (SWEDEN–CUBA), ANDERSSON (SWEDEN–CUBA)

PENALTIES
4: 3 SCORED, 1 MISSED

DREAM TEAM 1938

1950 BRAZIL

MARACANÃ STADIUM, WITNESS OF ONE OF THE WORST DEFEAT IN BRAZILIAN SOCCER HISTORY

1950 BRAZIL

Brazil hosted the World Cup from June 24 to July 16, 1950. They emerged from World War II relatively safe. Germany and Japan could not participate because of the result of the War. On the other hand, England, soccer's motherland, played for the first time. The Maracanã Stadium, which was built especially for the occasion, was shown to the world. It offered space for 200,000 fans.

13 teams out of 34 attended the Cup. The others cancelled their participation. India did not attend because their players were not allowed to play barefoot. Italy was devastated by a plane accident that killed all players of CA Torino. However the defending champions were persuaded to participate in the tournament.

For the first time, it was decided to play the competition in groups. For England, the first stage was a disaster. As pioneers of modern soccer, the British had previously disregarded all international tournaments with arrogance. They began with a deceptive 2-0 victory over Chile, but later they were defeated by the 'amateurs' from the USA. The coup de grâce was applied by Spain, who beat them 1-0. England was knocked out of the Cup.

Brazil was enjoying a good moment with several victories and faced Uruguay that was not in their best form in their previous matches. Everything indicated that Brazil was the favorite.

The passionate match was played in Maracanã. Brazilian players and fans were confident of a win. At halftime Brazil was leading 1-0, but in the second half Uruguay equalized and soon Alcides Ghiggia, the right winger, scored a goal that resulted in an overwhelming victory for the Uruguayan team. "Only three persons could silence the Maracanã with a single movement: Frank Sinatra, Pope John Paul II and me," said Ghiggia some time ago, at the age of 86.

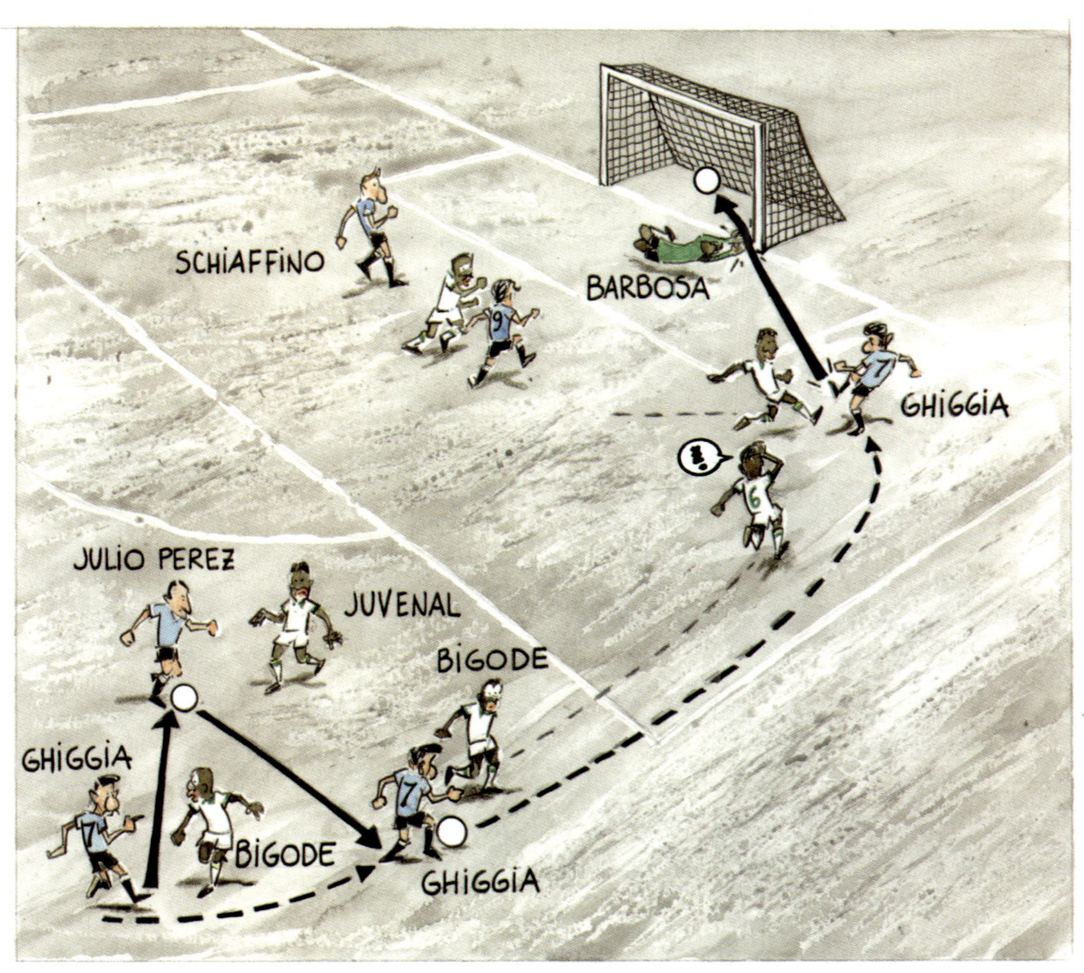

THE VICTORY OF URUGUAY OVER BRAZIL IS CALLED 'MARACANAZO'. HERE THE FINAL GOAL WAS SCORED BY GHIGGIA

ENGLISH PLAYERS WATCH WITH SURPRISE THE HIGH LEVEL OF SOCCER IN COPACABANA

ALF RAMSEY STARES IN DESPAIR AT JOE GAETJENS AS HE SCORES THE ONLY GOAL IN SPAIN'S SHOCKING UPSET OVER ENGLAND...

ADEMIR WON THE GOLDEN BOOT AS THE TOP SCORER IN THE COMPETITION (EIGHT GOALS), BUT COULD NOT WIN THE WORLD CUP

ALTHOUGH 174,000 TICKETS WERE SOLD FOR THE FINAL MATCH BETWEEN URUGUAY AND BRAZIL, ABOUT 30,000 GOT IN THE STADIUM WITHOUT TICKETS. FORTUNATELY, NO ONE WAS HURT

1950 WORLD CHAMPIONS: URUGUAY. TOP: OBDULIO VARELA, JUAN LÓPEZ (COACH), EUSEBIO TEJERA, VÁZQUEZ (CO-TRAINER), SCHUBERT GAMBETTA, MATÍAS GONZÁLEZ, ROQUE GASTÓN MÁSPOLI, VÍCTOR ANDRADE. BOTTON: KIRCHBERG (MASSELR), ALCIDES GHIGGIA, JULIO PÉREZ, ÓSCAR MÍGUEZ, JUAN SCHIAFFINO, RUBÉN MORÁN, FIGOLI (CO-TRAINER)

MOTIVATIONAL WORDS OF URUGUAYAN CAPTAIN OBDULIO VARELA FOR HIS TEAM, BEFORE THE FINAL

THE FINAL 16TH JULY, 1950

URUGUAY 2:1 BRAZIL

MARACANÃ STADIUM, RÍO DE JANEIRO
ATTENDANCE: 200,000
REFEREE: GEORGE READER (ENGLAND)

JUAN LÓPEZ, URUGUAYAN COACH SAID, "FELLOWS, IF WE RESPECT THEM, THEY´LL MAKE A CLEAN SWEEP, SO LET´S WIN THIS GAME"

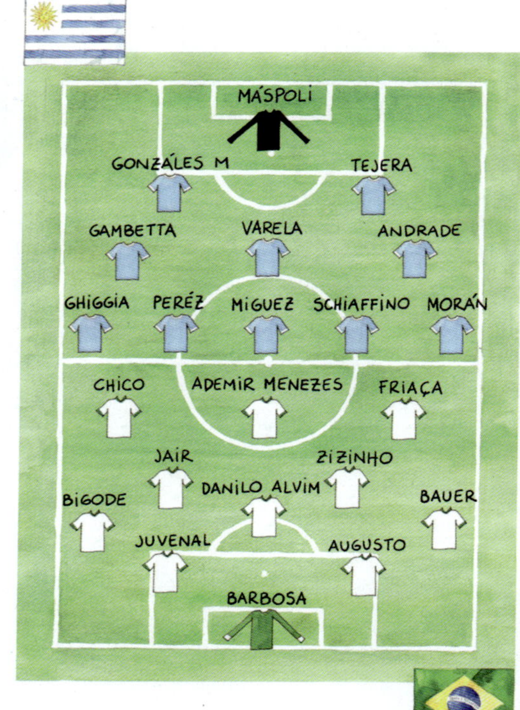

0:1
FRIAÇA (RIGHT) SCORES
47TH MINUTE

1:1
SCHIAFFINO VOLLEY
66TH MINUTE

2:1
GHIGGIA DRIBBLES THROUGH AND KICKS...
79TH MINUTE
1

...INTO THE BOTTOM CORNER
2

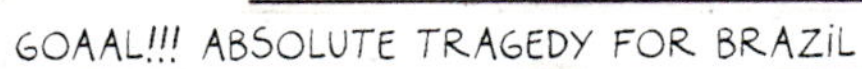
GOAAL!!! ABSOLUTE TRAGEDY FOR BRAZIL

3
URUGUAY CHAMPION

THERE WAS NO OFFICIAL CEREMONY PLANNED TO HAND OVER THE CUP TO URUGUAY...
...THEY CELEBRATED IN THE DRESSING ROOM

1950 IN OVERVIEW

GROUP 1

DATE	TEAM	R	TEAM
24.06.	BRAZIL	4:0	MEXICO
25.06.	YUGOSLAVIA	3:0	SWITZERLAND
28.06.	BRAZIL	2:2	SWITZERLAND
28.06.	YUGOSLAVIA	4:1	MEXICO
01.07.	BRAZIL	2:0	YUGOSLAVIA
02.07.	SWITZERLAND	2:1	MEXICO

PTS: BRAZIL 5, YUGOSLAVIA 4, SWITZERLAND 3, MEXICO 0

GROUP 2

DATE	TEAM	R	TEAM
25.06.	ENGLAND	2:0	CHILE
25.06.	SPAIN	3:1	USA
29.06.	SPAIN	2:0	CHILE
29.06.	USA	1:0	ENGLAND
02.07.	SPAIN	1:0	ENGLAND
02.07.	CHILE	5:2	USA

PTS: SPAIN 6, ENGLAND 2, CHILE 2, USA 2

GROUP 3

DATE	TEAM	R	TEAM
25.06.	SWEDEN	3:2	ITALY
29.06.	SWEDEN	2:2	PARAGUAY
02.07.	ITALY	2:0	PARAGUAY

PTS: SWEDEN 3, ITALY 2, PARAGUAY 1

GROUP 4

DATE	TEAM	R	TEAM
02.07.	URUGUAY	8:0	BOLIVIA

PTS: URUGUAY 2, BOLIVIA 0

FINAL ROUND

DATE	TEAM	R	TEAM
09.07.	URUGUAY	2:2	SPAIN
09.07.	BRAZIL	7:1	SWEDEN
13.07.	BRAZIL	6:1	SPAIN
13.07.	URUGUAY	3:2	SWEDEN
16.07.	SWEDEN	3:1	SPAIN
16.07.	URUGUAY	2:1	BRAZIL

PTS: URUGUAY 5, BRAZIL 4, SWEDEN 2, SPAIN 1

FINAL

DATE	TEAM	R	TEAM
16.07.	URUGUAY	2:1	BRAZIL

TICKET 1950

GHIGGIA, "THE GOAL OF VICTORY"

CHAMPION: URUGUAY

QUALIFIED TEAMS
13 (FROM 34 CANDIDATES)

PERIOD
24TH JUNE 1950–16TH JULY 1950

ATTENDANCE
1,045,246 (Ø: 47,511 PER MATCH)

PLAYERS IN FIELD

190

GOALS
88 (Ø: 4 PER MATCH)

OWN GOALS
1

FASTEST GOAL
2 MINUTES: ALFREDO (BRAZIL–SWITZERLAND)

MATCHES
22

MOST DANGEROUS TEAM
BRAZIL: 22 GOALS IN 6 MATCHES

TOP SCORERS
8 GOALS: ADEMIR (BRAZIL)
5 GOALS: MÍGUEZ (URUGUAY)
4 GOALS: BASORA, ZARRA (BOTH SPAIN), CHICO (BRAZIL) GHIGGIA (URUGUAY)

EXPULSIONS
0

BEST PLAYER TOP 3
1. ADEMIR (BRAZIL)
2. ALCIDES GHIGGIA (URUGUAY)
3. OBDULIO VARELA (URUGUAY)

BEST GOALKEEPER
ROQUE MÁSPOLI (URUGUAY)

3 OR MORE GOALS IN A MATCH
4 GOALS: ADEMIR (BRAZIL–SWEDEN)
3 GOALS: CREMASCHI (CHILE–USA)

PENALTIES
3: ALL SCORED

DREAM TEAM 1950

1954 SWITZERLAND

'WUNDER FROM BERN' (THE MIRACLE OF BERNE). GERMANY BEATS HUNGARY 3-2 UNDER THE RAIN

1954 SWITZERLAND

"Over! Over! Over! The match is over! Germany is world champion," shouted Herbert Zimmerman, German radio reporter. This famous phrase is the symbol of the Switzerland World Cup as well as the end of post-war depression in Germany. The so-called 'Miracle of Berne' is considered unofficially the birth certificate of the Federal Republic of Germany.

Nobody had imagined Germany as the World Champions in 1954. Hungary, which was in the same group, was considered the strongest team in the world. The Magical Magyars had won the Olympic Games and remained unbeaten in 31 consecutive matches since May 14, 1950. On their way to the final, Ferenc Puskás, Sándor Kocsis and their teammates had scored 25 goals in four matches.

But it wasn't only Hungary that was obsessed with scoring goals: with 140 goals in 26 matches, the 1954 World Cup became the highest-scoring tournament in history, averaging 5.4 goals per game. The Switzerland-Austria match (5-7), with 12 goals, still holds the record. Furthermore, this tournament was the first in which players wore numbers on their backs.

Germany was defeated by Hungary 8-3, but kept its place in the Cup due to two victories against Turkey. Hungary and Brazil played one of the most brutal matches in the quarter-finals. The violence in the field continued in the dressing rooms after Hungary´s victory 4-2.

Germany hammered Austria 6-1, paving the way to the final against Hungary. Under a heavy rain in Wankdorf Stadium in Berne, Puskás and Czibor put their country in front with just six minutes gone, but soon, thanks to Morlock and Rahn, Germany secured the equalizer. Six minutes before the final whistle, reporter Zimmerman´s words resounded, "Rahn has to shoot from distance... Rahn shoots! Goal! 3-2 to Germany!" The champions were awarded 1,000 Marks each, along with a motorcycle, baskets with food and... a TV set!

FERENC PUSKÁS FROM HUNGARY WAS SUPPOSED TO BE THE STAR OF THE CUP BUT AN INJURY STOPPED HIM FROM PLAYING BRILLIANTLY

(ABOVE) CAPTAIN FRITZ WALTER RECEIVES THE PRECIOUS TROPHY. (BELLOW) WALTER, ECKEL AND COACH HERBERGER ARE CARRIED ON FANS SHOULDERS. GERMANY HAD ACHIEVED A MIRACLE

HELMUT RAHN

SCORED TWO TIMES IN THE FINAL...

FRITZ WALTER, CAPTAIN OF GERMAN TEAM

...INCLUDING HIS LATE WINNER

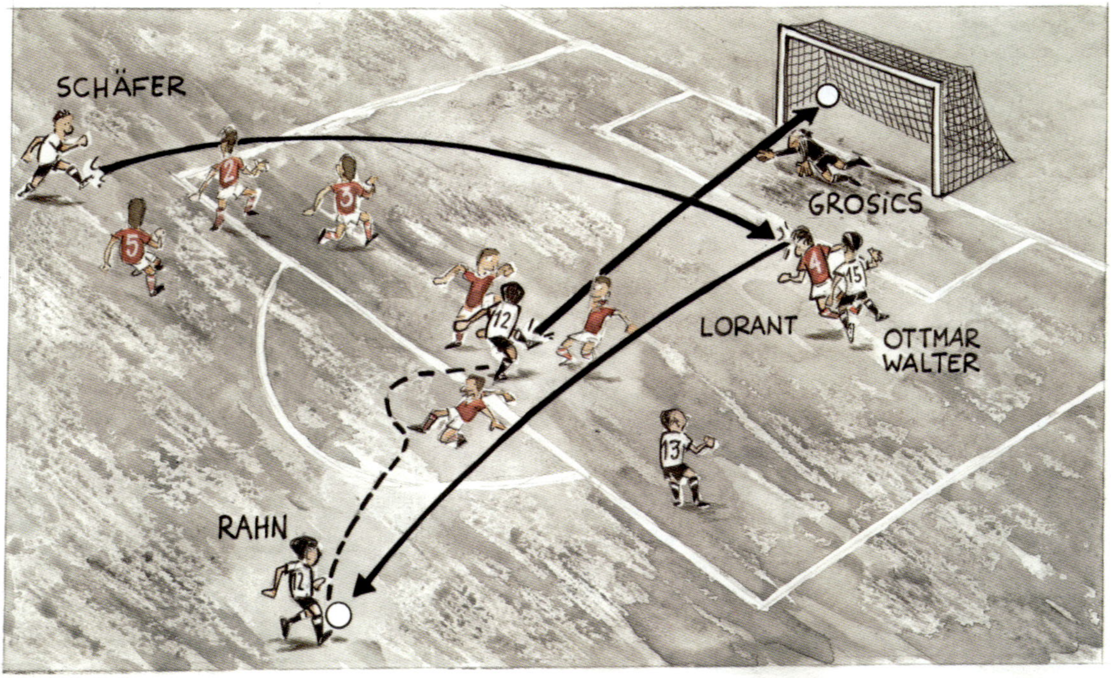

1954

TOP SCORER KOCSIS FROM HUNGARY, WHO SCORED 11 GOALS WAS PART OF THE MOST SUCCESFUL TEAM IN HUNGARIAN HISTORY. ALMOST UNBEATABLE, WITH 31 MATCHES WON, HUNGARY CONCEDED THE FINAL GAME

GERMAN ENTREPRENEUR ADI DASSLER (ADIDAS) INVENTED SCREW-IN STUDS FOR HIS NATIONAL TEAM. THEY HOPED FOR RAIN IN THE FINAL...

...AND THEIR DREAM CAME TRUE!

2
3

1954 WORLD CHAMPIONS: WEST GERMANY. TOP: SEPP HERBERGER (COACH),
FRITZ WALTER, HELMUT RAHN, JUPP POSIPAL, HORST ECKEL, WERNER LIEBRICH, OTTMAR WALTE
HANS SCHÄFER, MAX MORLOCK. BOTTOM: KARL MAX, TONI TUREK, WERNER KOHLMEYER

GERMAN RADIO REPORTER HERBERT ZIMMERMANN BECAME FAMOUS FOR HIS COMMENTARY IN THE FINAL. THE CUP WAS THE FIRST TO BE TELEVISED, GIVING EVERYONE THE POSSIBILITY TO BE PART OF SOCCER SINCE THEN

THE FINAL 4TH JULY, 1954

WEST GERMANY 3:2 HUNGARY

WANKDORF STADIUM, BERN

ATTENDANCE: 64,000

REFEREE: WILLIAM LING (ENGLAND)

"IF IT RAINS, WE HAVE AN ADVANTAGE OVER HUNGARY. WE PLAY WITH SCREW-IN STUDS AND THEIR LEGS WILL BE HEAVY"

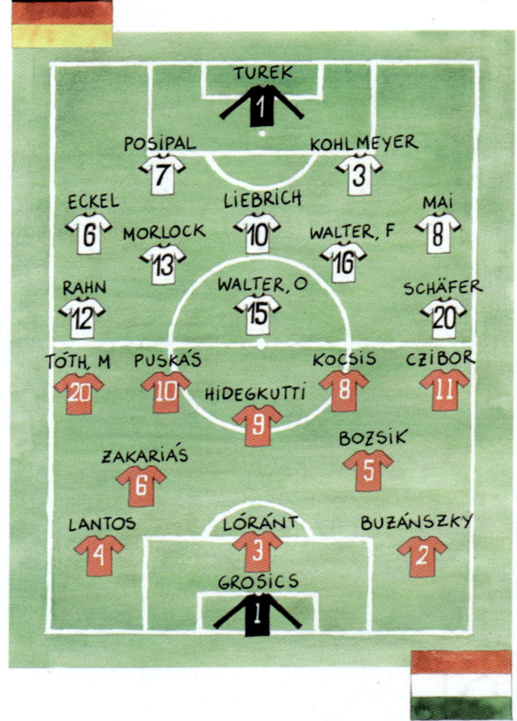

6TH MINUTE

8TH MINUTE

0:2 CZIBOR TAKES ADVANTAGE OF TUREK AND KOHLMEYER'S MISUNDERSTANDING

84TH MINUTE

HELMUT RAHN KICKS AND LEADS GERMANY TO VICTORY

1954 IN OVERVIEW

GROUP 1

DATE	TEAM	R	TEAM
16.06.	YUGOSLAVIA	1:0	FRANCE
16.06.	BRAZIL	5:0	MEXICO
19.06.	BRAZIL	1:1	YUGOSLAVIA
19.06.	FRANCE	3:2	MEXICO

PTS: BRAZIL 3, YUGOSLAVIA 3, FRANCE 2, MEXICO 0

GROUP 2

DATE	TEAM	R	TEAM
17.06.	WEST GERMANY	4:1	TURKEY
17.06.	HUNGARY	9:0	SOUTH KOREA
20.06.	HUNGARY	8:3	WEST GERMANY
20.06.	TURKEY	7:0	SOUTH KOREA
*23.06.	WEST GERMANY	7:2	TURKEY

PTS: HUNGARY 4, WEST GERMANY 2, TURKEY 2, SOUTH KOREA 0
* REPLAY MATCH

GROUP 3

DATE	TEAM	R	TEAM
16.06.	AUSTRIA	1:0	SCOTLAND
16.06.	URUGUAY	2:0	CZECHOSLOVAKIA
19.06.	URUGUAY	7:0	SCOTLAND
19.06.	AUSTRIA	5:0	CZECHOSLOVAKIA

PTS: URUGUAY 4, AUSTRIA 4, CZECHOSLOVAKIA 0, SCOTLAND 0

GROUP 4

DATE	TEAM	R	TEAM
17.06.	SWITZERLAND	2:1	ITALY
17.06.	ENGLAND	4:4	BELGIUM
20.06.	ITALY	4:1	BELGIUM
20.06.	ENGLAND	2:0	SWITZERLAND
23.06.	SWITZERLAND	4:1	ITALY

PTS: ENGLAND 3, SWITZERLAND 2, ITALY, 2, BELGIUM 1

QUARTER-FINALS

DATE	TEAM	R	TEAM
26.06.	AUSTRIA	7:5	SWITZERLAND
26.06.	URUGUAY	4:2	ENGLAND
27.06.	HUNGARY	4:2	BRAZIL
27.06.	W. GERMANY	2:0	YUGOSLAVIA

SEMIFINALS

DATE	TEAM	R	TEAM
30.06.	HUNGARY	4:2	URUGUAY
30.06.	W. GERMANY	6:1	AUSTRIA

3RD PLACE

DATE	TEAM	R	TEAM
03.07.	AUSTRIA	3:1	URUGUAY

FINAL

DATE	TEAM	R	TEAM
04.07.	W. GERMANY	3:2	HUNGARY

TICKET 1954

CHAMPION:
WEST GERMANY

RETURN OF BERN´S HEROS

QUALIFIED TEAMS
16 (FROM 38 CANDIDATES)

PERIOD
16 JUNE 1954–04 JULY 1954

ATTENDANCE
768,607 (Ø: 29,562 PER MATCH)

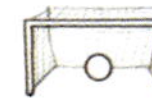

GOALS
140 (Ø: 5.38 PER MATCH)

PLAYERS IN FIELD
231

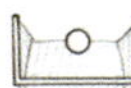

OWN GOALS
4

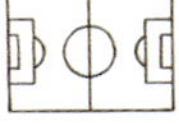

FASTEST GOAL
2 MINUTES: SUAT (TURKEY–WEST GERMANY, 1ST MATCH)

MATCHES
26

MOST DANGEROUS TEAM
HUNGARY: 27 GOALS IN 5 MATCHES

EXPULSIONS
3 (Ø: 0.12 PER MATCH)

TOP SCORERS
11 GOALS: KOCSIS (HUNGARY)
6 GOALS: MORLOCK (WEST GERMANY),
HÜGI (SWITZERLAND),
PROBST (AUSTRIA)

BEST PLAYER TOP 3
1. FERENC PUSKÁS (HUNGARY)
2. SANDOR KOCSIS (HUNGARY)
3. FRITZ WALTER, HELMUT RAHN (BOTH WEST GERMANY)

3 OR MORE GOALS IN A MATCH
4 GOALS: KOCSIS (HUNGARY–WEST GERMANY)
3 GOALS: KOCSIS (HUNGARY–SOUTH KOREA)
BURHAN (TURKEY–SOUTH KOREA),
HÜGI (SWITZERLAND–AUSTRIA),
WAGNER (AUSTRIA–SWITZERLAND),
MORLOCK (WEST GERMANY–TURKEY),
PROBST (AUSTRIA–CZECHOSLOVAKIA),
BORGES (URUGUAY–SCOTLAND)

PENALTIES
7: 6 SCORED, 1 MISSED

BEST GOALKEEPER
GYULA GROSICS (HUNGARY)

DREAM TEAM 1954

1958 SWEDEN

PELÉ, AT THE AGE OF 17 BECAME AN INTERNATIONAL STAR WHEN BRAZIL WON THE WORLD CUP FOR THE FIRST TIME

1958 SWEDEN

Pérola Negra (the black pearl), O Rei do Futebol (The King of Soccer), all those are great nicknames of a great player as Edson Arantes do Nascimento, who, at the age of seventeen, astonished the world of soccer. Famous for his name Pelé, he began his unprecedented career in this World Cup, and in 2000, he was named by FIFA as the "Player of the 20th Century" (an award he shared with Diego Maradona).

Pelé, who had been labelled as 'Immature' by the team psychologist, celebrated his international debut. Soviet Union and Great Britain participated in the tournament for the first time. The latter appeared with England, Scotland, Wales and Northern Ireland. 55 National Teams applied for the Cup, but only 14 qualified. Host Sweden and defending champion Germany qualified automatically. The great absentees were Italy and Spain, whereas the favorite was France. Their striker Just Fontaine scored four times against Germany in the match for the third place. A prolific forward, he is best known for being the record holder for most goals scored in a single edition of the FIFA World Cup (13 goals).

During the semifinals between Sweden and Germany, soccer showed its dark side. Insulting songs, violent words and xenophobia appeared in the match. After a series of violent conflicts on the field, Eric Juskowiak was the first player to be sent off in an international game. Among suspicions that the Hungarian referee favored the Swedish team, Sweden went through 3-1. This led to a growing tension that lasted many years after the match.

On the other hand, Pelé single-handedly eliminated France in the other semifinal. The hat-trick in the semifinal is one of the dazzling moments in his glorious career. During the Final, Brazilian spectators trembled in fear when Sweden scored within the first four minutes. Pelé scored twice and helped Brazil win the match 5-2! He became the first superstar of soccer.

FRENCH FORWARD JUST FONTAINE WON THE GOLDEN BOOT WITH 13 GOALS, STILL A TOURNAMENT RECORD

FONTAINE SCORED A GREAT GOAL AGAINST BRAZIL IN THE SEMIFINAL. BUT IT WAS NOT ENOUGH; THEY LOST 5–2

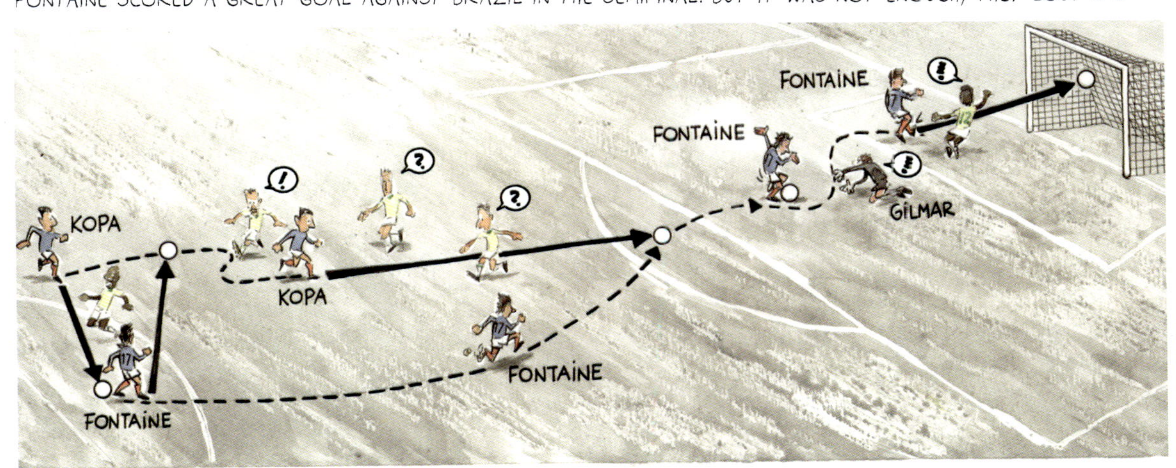

BRAZIL WAS SAVED BY A PELÉ'S GOAL AGAINST WALES

THE UNFORGETTABLE FIRST GOAL THAT PELÉ SCORED IN THE FINAL: CHEST TRAP AND CHIP SHOT WILL BE REMEMBERED FOR ETERNITY...

(RIGHT) EDSON ARANTES DO NASCIMENTO OR 'O REI' OR SIMPLY, PELÉ

10
O Rei Pelé
O REI PELÉ
10 10 10 10 10
10 10 10 10
O Rei Pelé O REI PELÉ
O Rei Pelé O Rei Pelé
O Rei Pelé O Rei Pelé
O Rei Pelé
O REI PELÉ,
O REI PELÉ,
O REI PELÉ,
O REI PELÉ
O Rei Pelé
O Rei Pelé
ACZEL

CBD
BRASIL

1958 WORLD CHAMPIONS: BRAZIL. TOP: VICENTE FEOLA (COACH), DJALMA SANTOS, ZITO, BELLINI, NILTON SANTOS, ORLANDO, GILMAR, BOTTOM: GARRINCHA, DIDI, PELÉ, VAVÁ, ZAGALLO, AMARAL (ASSISTANT COACH)

TENSION IN GOTHENBURG: GERMAN DEFENDER JUSKOWIAK GOES MAD AFTER THE RED CARD, SWEDEN WIN 3-1 AND ADVANCE TO THE FINAL

YOUNG PELÉ IN TEARS AFTER WINNING THE WORLD CUP

THE FINAL 29TH JUNE, 1958

SWEDEN 2:5 BRAZIL

RASUNDA STADIUM, SOLNA
ATTENDANCE: 51,800
REFEREE: MAURICE GUIGUE (FRANCE)

VICENTE FEOLA (BRAZIL COACH) AND HIS REVOLUTIONARY 4-2-4 SYSTEM

0:1
LIEDHOLM SCORES EARLY
4TH MINUTE
9TH MINUTE
1:1
VAVÁ
2:1
GARRINCHA CROSSES, VAVÁ SCORES
32ND MINUTE
3:1
PELÉ STOPS THE BALL WITH HIS CHEST
CHIPS...
...AND VOLLEYS A BRILLIANT GOAL!
FÖR HELA FA
4:1
ZAGALLO
68TH MINUTE
4:2
SIMONSSON
80TH MINUTE
5:2
PELÉ HEADER
90TH MINUTE
AT THE END OF THE GAME, PELÉ DOES NOT KNOW WHETHER TO CRY OR LAUGH BUT IT IS CERTAIN THAT A LEGEND IS BORN...
BRAZIL WORLD CHAMPION

1958 IN OVERVIEW

GROUP 1

DATE	TEAM	R	TEAM
08.06.	ARGENTINA	1:3	WEST GERMANY
08.06.	N. IRELAND	1:0	CZECHOSLOVAKIA
11.06.	ARGENTINA	3:1	N. IRELAND
11.06.	WEST GERMANY	2:2	CZECHOSLOVAKIA
15.06.	CZECHOSLOVAKIA	6:1	ARGENTINA
15.06.	WEST GERMANY	2:2	N. IRELAND
17.06.	N. IRELAND	2:1	CZECHOSLOVAKIA

PTS: W. GERMANY 4, N. IRELAND 3, CZECHOSLOVAKIA 3, ARGENTINA 2

GROUP 2

DATE	TEAM	R	TEAM
08.06.	YUGOSLAVIA	1:1	SCOTLAND
08.06.	FRANCE	7:3	PARAGUAY
11.06.	YUGOSLAVIA	3:2	FRANCE
11.06.	PARAGUAY	3:2	SCOTLAND
15.06.	PARAGUAY	3:3	YUGOSLAVIA
15.06.	FRANCE	2:1	SCOTLAND

PTS: FRANCE 4, YUGOSLAVIA 4, PARAGUAY 3, SCOTLAND 1

GROUP 3

DATE	TEAM	R	TEAM
08.06.	SWEDEN	3:0	MEXICO
08.06.	HUNGARY	1:1	WALES
11.06.	MEXICO	1:1	WALES
12.06.	SWEDEN	2:1	HUNGARY
15.06.	SWEDEN	0:0	WALES
15.06.	HUNGARY	4:0	MEXICO
17.06.	WALES	2:1	HUNGARY

PTS: SWEDEN 5, WALES 3, HUNGARY 3, MEXICO 1

GROUP 4

DATE	TEAM	R	TEAM
08.06.	USSR	2:2	ENGLAND
08.06.	BRAZIL	3:0	AUSTRIA
11.06.	USSR	2:0	AUSTRIA
11.06.	BRAZIL	0:0	ENGLAND
15.06.	BRAZIL	2:0	USSR
15.06.	ENGLAND	2:2	AUSTRIA
17.06.	USSR	1:0	ENGLAND

PTS: BRAZIL 5, USSR 3, ENGLAND 3, AUSTRIA 1

QUARTER-FINALS

DATE	TEAM	R	TEAM
19.06.	BRAZIL	1:0	WALES
19.06.	FRANCE	4:0	N. IRELAND
19.06.	W. GERMANY	1:0	YUGOSLAVIA
19.06.	SWEDEN	2:0	USSR

SEMIFINALS

DATE	TEAM	R	TEAM
24.06.	SWEDEN	3:1	W. GERMANY
24.06.	BRAZIL	5:2	FRANCE

3RD PLACE

DATE	TEAM	R	TEAM
28.06.	FRANCE	6:3	W. GERMANY

FINAL

DATE	TEAM	R	TEAM
29.06.	BRAZIL	5:2	SWEDEN

TICKET 1958

CHAMPION:
BRAZIL

PELÉ'S SIGNATURE

QUALIFIED TEAMS
16 (FROM 52 CANDIDATES)

PERIOD
8TH JUNE, 1958–29TH JUNE, 1958

ATTENDANCE
819,810 (Ø: 23,423 PER MATCH)

GOALS
126 (Ø: 3.6 PER MATCH)

PLAYERS IN FIELD
246

OWN GOALS
0

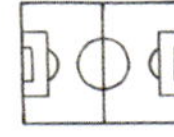

FASTEST GOAL
75 SECONDS: VAVÁ (BRAZIL–FRANCE)

MATCHES
35

MOST MOST DANGEROUS TEAM
FRANCE: 23 GOALS IN 6 MATCHES

TOP SCORERS
13 GOALS: FONTAINE (FRANCE)
6 GOALS: RAHN (WEST GERMANY), PELÉ (BRAZIL)

EXPULSIONS
3 (Ø: 0.09 PER MATCH)

BEST PLAYER TOP 3
1. DIDI (BRAZIL)
2. JUST FONTAINE (FRANCE)
3. PELÉ (BRAZIL)

3 OR MORE GOALS IN A MATCH
4 GOALS: FONTAINE (FRANCE–WEST GERMANY)
3 GOALS: FONTAINE (FRANCE–PARAGUAY), PELÉ (BRAZIL–FRANCE)

BEST GOALKEEPER
HARRY GREGG (N. IRELAND)

PENALTIES
8: 7 SCORED, 1 MISSED

BEST YOUNG PLAYER
PELÉ, 17 YEARS (BRAZIL)

DREAM TEAM 1958

1962 CHILE

GARRINCHA FOOLS THE OPPONENT DEFENDERS AND BRAZIL SEALS THE SECOND WORLD TITLE

1962 CHILE

There were 56 teams ready to participate, which represented a new record, but only 16, from Europe, Central America and South America qualified for the final stages.
1962 World Cup was one of the most brutal tournaments ever seen. It took place in Chile between May 30 and June 17.

During the early stages, the players showed reckless and violent behaviour that reached its highest point in 'The Battle of Santiago,' where players of Chile and Italy were involved in a sad and violent fight. Fans from all over the world watched the show on their televisions in disbelief. Two players from Italy were sent off; a player from Chile broke Umberto Maschio's nose with a left hook. There were police interventions on the field, as well as kicks and punches. Chile won 2-0, and it was called by the BBC "the most stupid, appalling, disgusting and disgraceful exhibition of soccer."

Uwe Seeler was the top scorer of Germany, but he could not avoid defeat against Yugoslavia 0-1 in the quarter-finals.

The best Argentine player of that era, Alfredo Di Stéfano (the Real Madrid star), was also present, playing for Spain, although his team did not go far in the tournament.

Brazil had to do mostly without Pelé who limped out of the second game due to an injury to his left thigh. This made him watch the rest of the tournament from the bench. Mané Garrincha — nicknamed "The Little Bird" — wearing the number 7 shirt, whose left leg was 6 centimetres shorter than the other, carried the enormous responsibility of leading the team in Pelé's absence. He was the star of Brazil's campaign, scoring two goals in the semifinal against Chile (4–2). Although he had been sent off, he was allowed to play in the final against Czechoslovakia. Although he did not score in the final, two mistakes by the Czech goalkeeper helped Brazil win 3–1 and retain the World Cup title.

THE BATTLE OF SANTIAGO

'THE BATTLE OF SANTIAGO': ALTHOUGH LEONEL SANCHEZ FROM CHILE PUNCHED TWO ITALIAN PLAYERS, IT WAS THE AZURRI (GIORGI FERRINI AND MARIO DAVID) WHO WERE SENT OFF. CHILE WON 2-0 AND THE ENGLISH REFEREE KEN ASTON DEFINED THE GAME AS 'UNCONTROLLABLE'

PELÉ LEAVES THE FIELD WITH AN INJURED LEG. AMARILDO REPLACED HIM BUT THE BRAZILIAN SHOW WOULD CONTINUE WITH GARRINCHA

ENGLISH FORWARD JIMMY GREAVES WAS INVOLVED IN A FUNNY SITUATION WHEN CAUGHT BY A STRAY DOG DURING THE GAME WITH BRAZIL. GARRINCHA TOOK THE DOG HOME AS A PET

AMAZING SKILLS, DISGUISE, NUTMEG. GARRINCHA, DID NOT STOP FOOLING HIS OPPONENTS. HE IS CONSIDERED THE BEST RIGHT WINGER IN THE HISTORY OF SOCCER. HE HAD A CROOKED SPINE...

...AND THE LEFT LEG A COUPLE OF INCHES SHORTER THAN HIS RIGHT

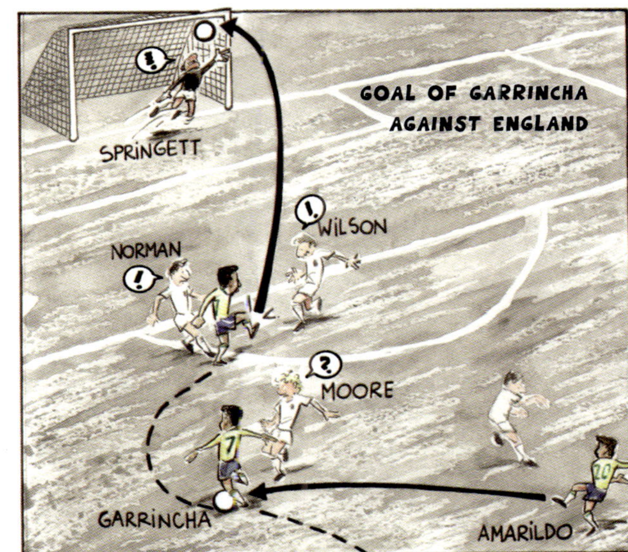

THE SHOW OF GARRINCHA

NOTHING IN MY POCKETS, NOTHING UP MY SLEEVES...
TYPICAL GARRINCHA FEINTS WITHOUT BALL

1962 WORLD CHAMPIONS: BRAZIL. TOP: AYMORE MOREIRA (COACH), DJALMA SANTOS, ZITO, GILMAR, ZOZIMO, NILTON SANTOS, MAURO, DR. GOSLING (TEAM DOCTOR). BOTTOM: AMÉRICO (MASSEUR), GARRINCHA, DIDI, VAVÁ, AMARILDO, ZAGALLO, AN ASSISTANT MANAGER

GARRINCHA AND FIVE OTHER PLAYERS SHARED THE GOLDEN BOOT (FOUR GOALS EACH). LEONEL SÁNCHEZ (CHILE), DRAAN JERKOVI (YUGOSLAVIA), VALENTIN IVANOV (SOVIET UNION), FLORIAN ALBERT (HUNGARY) AND VAVÁ FROM BRAZIL

THE FINAL 17TH JUNE, 1962

BRAZIL 3:1 CZECHOSLOVAKIA

ESTADIO NACIONAL, SANTIAGO
ATTENDANCE: 68,000
REFEREE: NIKOLAI LATYSCHEV (SOVIET UNION)

AYMORE MOREIRA, BRAZILIAN COACH, HAD A SIMPLE PHILOSOPHY, BUT CHANGED THE SYSTEM FROM 4-2-4 TO 4-3-3

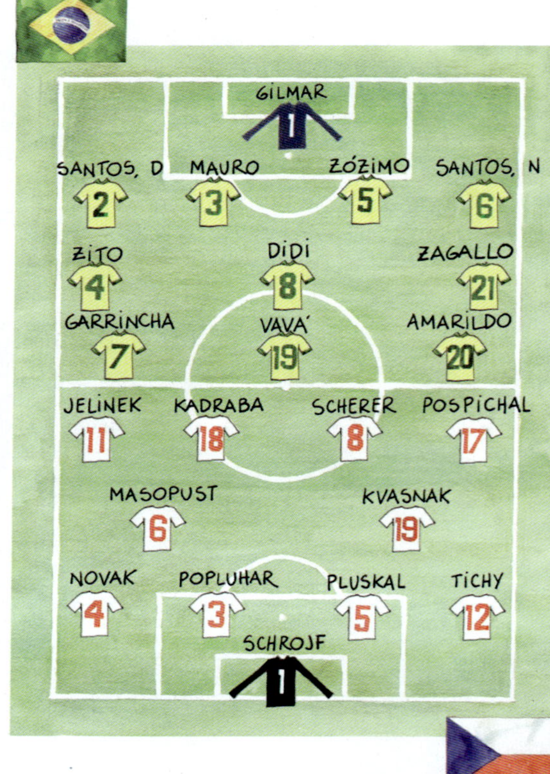

PELÉ
CAN WATCH,
BUT NOT
PLAY

0:1
MASOPUST
15TH MINUTE

1:1
AMARILDO EQUALISES FROM AN IMPOSSIBLE ANGLE
17TH MINUTE

2:1
ZITO HEADS HOME AMARILDO'S CROSS
69TH MINUTE

3:1
VAVÁ TAKES ADVANTAGE OF THE GOALKEEPER'S MISTAKE AND SCORES.
BRAZIL CHAMPION!!!
78TH MINUTE

1962 IN OVERVIEW

GROUP 1

DATE	TEAM	R	TEAM
30.05.	URUGUAY	2:1	COLOMBIA
31.05.	USSR	2:0	YUGOSLAVIA
02.06.	YUGOSLAVIA	3:1	URUGUAY
03.06.	USSR	4:4	COLOMBIA
06.06.	USSR	2:1	URUGUAY
07.06.	YUGOSLAVIA	5:0	COLOMBIA

PTS: USSR 5, YUGOSLAVIA 4, URUGUAY 2, COLOMBIA 1

GROUP 2

DATE	TEAM	R	TEAM
30.05.	CHILE	3:1	SWITZERLAND
31.05.	WEST GERMANY	0:0	ITALY
02.06.	CHILE	2:0	ITALY
03.06.	WEST GERMANY	2:1	SWITZERLAND
06.06.	WEST GERMANY	2:0	CHILE
07.06.	ITALY	3:0	SWITZERLAND

PTS: WEST GERMANY 5, CHILE 4, ITALY 3, SWITZERLAND 0

GROUP 3

DATE	TEAM	R	TEAM
30.05.	BRAZIL	2:0	MEXICO
31.05.	CZECHOSL.	1:0	SPAIN
02.06.	BRAZIL	0:0	CZECHOSL.
03.06.	SPAIN	1:0	MEXICO
06.06.	BRAZIL	2:1	SPAIN
07.06.	MEXICO	3:1	CZECHOSL.

PTS: BRAZIL 5, CZECHOSLOVAKIA 3, MEXICO 2, SPAIN 2

GROUP 4

DATE	TEAM	R	TEAM
30.05.	ARGENTINA	1:0	BULGARIA
31.05.	HUNGARY	2:1	ENGLAND
02.06.	ENGLAND	3:1	ARGENTINA
03.06.	HUNGARY	6:1	BULGARIA
06.06.	HUNGARY	0:0	ARGENTINA
07.06.	ENGLAND	0:0	BULGARIA

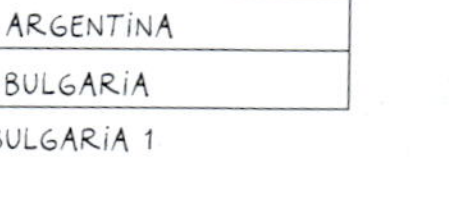

PTS: HUNGARY 5, ENGLAND 3, ARGENTINA 3, BULGARIA 1

QUARTER-FINALS

DATE	TEAM	R	TEAM
10.06.	BRAZIL	3:1	ENGLAND
10.06.	CHILE	2:1	USSR
10.06.	YUGOSLAVIA	1:0	W. GERMANY
10.06.	CZECHOSL.	1:0	HUNGARY

SEMIFINALS

DATE	TEAM	R	TEAM
13.06.	CZECHOSL.	3:1	YUGOSLAVIA
13.06.	BRAZIL	4:2	CHILE

3RD PLACE

DATE	TEAM	R	TEAM
16.06.	CHILE	1:0	YUGOSLAVIA

FINAL

DATE	TEAM	R	TEAM
17.06.	BRAZIL	3:1	CZECHOSL.

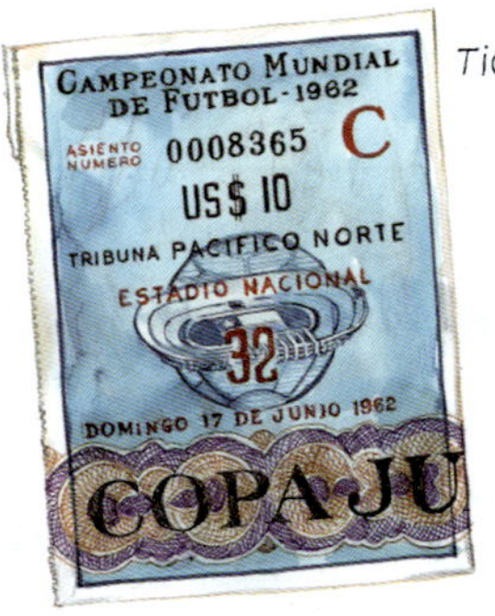

TICKET 1962

A HARD WORK: I.D OF THE REFEREE FROM 'THE BATTLE OF SANTIAGO'

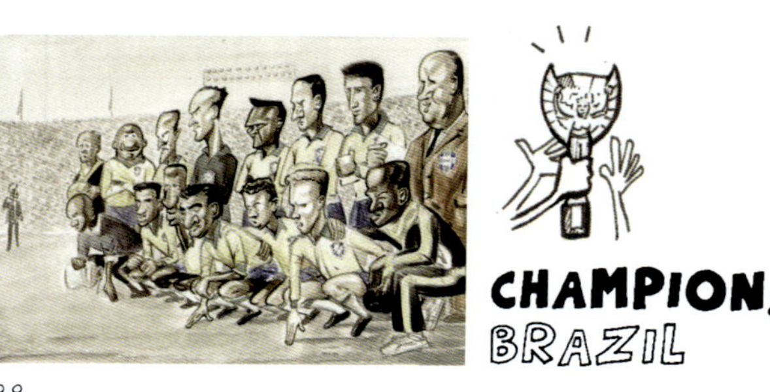

CHAMPION: BRAZIL

QUALIFIED TEAMS
16 (FROM 54CANDIDATES)

PERIOD
30TH MAY, 1962–17TH JUNE, 1962

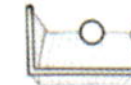

ATTENDANCE
893,172 (Ø: 27,912 PER MATCH)

PLAYERS IN FIELD

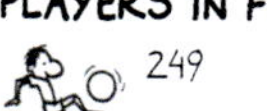

249

GOALS
89 (Ø: 2.78 PER MATCH)

OWN GOALS
0

FASTEST GOAL
16 SECONDS: MASEK
(CZECHOSLOVAKIA–MEXICO)

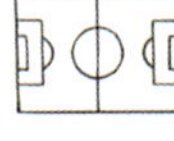

MATCHES
32

MOST DANGEROUS TEAM
BRAZIL: 14 GOALS IN 6 MATCHES

TOP SCORERS
4 GOALS: IVANOV (USSR)
SANCHEZ (CHILE), GARRINCHA, VAVÁ
(BOTH BRAZIL), ALBERT (HUNGARY),
JERKOVI (YUGOSLAVIA)

EXPULSIONS
6 (Ø: 0.19 PER MATCH)

BEST PLAYER TOP 3
1. GARRINCHA (BRAZIL)
2. JOSEF MASOPUST (CZECHOSLOVAKIA)
3. VAVÁ (BRAZIL)

BEST GOALKEEPER
VILIAM SCHROJF
(CZECHOSLOVAKIA)

3 OR MORE GOALS IN A MATCH
3 GOALS: ALBERT (HUNGARY–BULGARIA)

PENALTIES
9: ALL SCORED

BEST YOUNG PLAYER
FLORIAN ALBERT,
20 YEARS (HUNGARY)

DREAM TEAM 1962

1966 ENGLAND

AT LAST ENGLAND
WORLD CHAMPIONS!!!
THE CREATORS OF THE GAME
ACHIEVED VICTORY

1966 ENGLAND

Did the ball cross the line or not? The goal in the 1966 Final at Wembley has been debated fiercely ever since. The World Cup in England, from July 11 to 30, was full of emotions and surprises. Fortunately, a dog managed to recover the stolen trophy, allowing it to be handed to the World Champions by the Queen. "Soccer is coming home!"

A new record was reached with 71 national teams playing qualifications. Portugal and North Korea, whose teams had only started playing two years before qualifying for the tournament, surprised everyone with their performances. In the group stage, North Korea eliminated Italy and almost repeated the feat against Portugal in the quarter-finals, but Eusébio scored four goals to turn the game around (5–3).

The unfair sending-off of Antonio Rattín in the quarterfinals against England marked Argentina's elimination, caused an international scandal, and fueled the historic rivalry between the two countries. On the other hand, Brazil was eliminated in the first stage; without Pelé, who was injured again and had to be sidelined, it ended the South American team's chances.

The trophy was stolen and caused commotion, but Pickles, a small black-and-white dog, calmed everyone down by finding it in a park in London.

In the semifinals, Beckenbauer and Helmut Haller led West Germany to a 2–1 victory over the Soviet Union, while England defeated Portugal 2–1 thanks to two goals by Bobby Charlton, clearing the path to Wembley. In the final, after 90 minutes, the two teams were tied 2–2. In the 101st minute, Geoff Hurst's shot hit the crossbar, bounced down, and, according to the referee, crossed the line. It is still debated, but the goal was awarded. On a counterattack, Bobby Moore took the ball out of the defence and passed it to Hurst, who sent it into the back of the net. The match ended 4–2. The pictures in which German star Uwe Seeler leaves the field with his head down will always be an icon of this final. England won the World Cup for the first and only time to date.

GEOFF HURST SHOOTS, THE BALL HITS THE CROSSBAR AND DOES IT CROSS THE LINE OR NOT? THAT'S BEEN ARGUED EVER SINCE AND BECAME THE FAMOUS "WAS IT OVER THE LINE?" GOAL OF ALL TIME

PICKLES (THE DOG, NOT THE PHOTOGRAPHER) BECAME THE HERO OF THE DAY WHEN HE FOUND THE STOLEN TROPHY IN A GARDEN IN SOUTH-EAST LONDON

BOBBY CHARLTON SCORES THE FIRST GOAL FOR ENGLAND IN THE COMPETITION DURING THE MATCH AGAINST MEXICO

EUSEBIO WON THE GOLDEN BOOT WITH NINE GOALS, FOUR OF WHICH SCORED DURING THE MATCH AGAINST NORTH KOREA AS HE PULLED HIS TEAM BACK FROM A 3-0 DEFICIT, PORTUGAL FINALLY WON 5-3

PAK DOO IK SCORED THE GOAL THAT CAUSED A SENSATION, WHEN NORTH KOREA, WINNING 1-0, FORCED ITALY TO GO HOME AFTER THE GROUP STAGE

ENGLAND COACH ALF RAMSEY STOPS GEORGE COHEN WHEN HE WAS EXCHANGING SHIRTS AFTER THE QUARTER-FINAL WITH ARGENTINA. RAMSEY CALLED THE SOUTH-AMERICANS 'ANIMALS'

MEXICAN GOALKEEPER ANTONIO CARBAJAL MADE HISTORY AFTER PLAYING IN HIS FIFTH WORLD CUP

UFF!
PELÉ'S WORLD CUP WAS OVER QUICKLY AFTER THE BRUTAL FOULS COMMITTED AGAINST HIM BY PLAYERS FROM BULGARIA AND PORTUGAL

BOBBY CHARLTON'S GOAL AGAINST PORTUGAL IN THE SEMIFINAL, AFTER A BRILLIANT TEAM MOVE

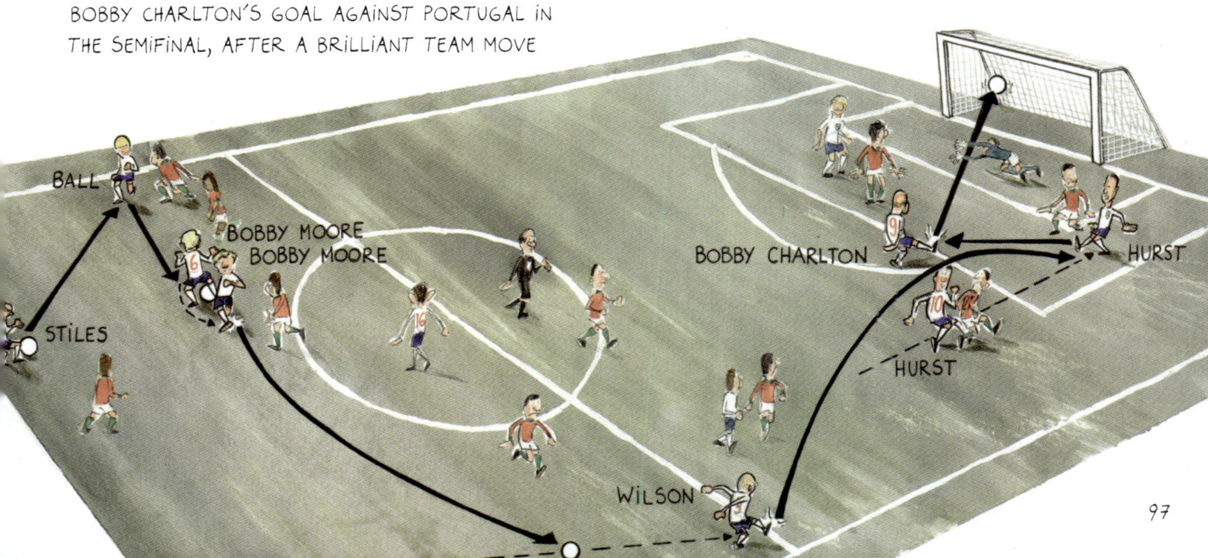

1966 WORLD CHAMPIONS: ENGLAND.
TOP: HAROLD SHEPHERDSON (TRAINER), NOBBY STILES, ROGER HUNT, GORDON BANKS, JACK CHARLTON, GEORGE COHEN, RAY WILSON, ALF RAMSEY (COACH)
BOTTOM: MARTIN PETERS, GEOFF HURST, BOBBY MOORE, ALAN BALL, BOBBY CHARLTO

EVEN STRONG MEN WEEP. JACKIE CHARLTON SINKS TO THE TURF AFTER HIS TEAMS VICTORY

ENGLAND'S COACH RAMSEY WAS FAMOUS FOR HIS PHLEGMATIC CHARACTER. AT THE FINAL WHISTLE HE SAT MOTIONLESS AND TOLD HIS ASSISTANT HAROLD SHEPHERDSON: "SIT DOWN HAROLD, YOU'RE BLOCKING MY VIEW" AS HAROLD JUMPED FOR JOY.
GERMAN MANAGER HELMUT SCHÖN (LEFT) COULD NOT BELIEVE HIS TEAM HAD LOST

THE FINAL 30TH JULY, 1966

ENGLAND 4:2 WEST GERMANY (EXTRA-TIME)

WEMBLEY STADIUM, LONDON

ATTENDANCE: 98,000

REFEREE: GOTTFRIED DIENST (SWITZERLAND)

LINEMAN:
TOFIK BACHRAMOW (USSR)

ALF RAMSEY, ENGLAND'S COACH

0:1
HALLER SCORES FIRST
12TH MINUTE
1:1
HURST, HEADER
18TH MINUTE
2:1
PETERS
78TH MINUTE
2:2
WEBER
90TH MINUTE
3:2
HURST...BUT DID THE BALL CROSS THE LINE OR NOT?
EXTRA-TIME
101ST MINUTE
THE RUSS AN LINESMAN WAS SURE THE BALL CROSSED THE LINE AND THE REFEREE AGREED...
GOAL
...PROTESTS DID NOT CHANGE HIS MIND
4:2
HURST'S HAT-TRICK
120TH MINUTE
ENGLAND WORLD CHAMPION!!!

1966 IN OVERVIEW

GROUP 1

DATE	TEAM	R	TEAM
11.07.	ENGLAND	0:0	URUGUAY
13.07.	FRANCE	1:1	MEXICO
15.07.	URUGUAY	2:1	FRANCE
16.07.	ENGLAND	2:0	MEXICO
19.07.	URUGUAY	0:0	MEXICO
20.07.	ENGLAND	2:0	FRANCE

PTS: ENGLAND 5, URUGUAY 4, MEXICO 2, FRANCE 1

GROUP 2

DATE	TEAM	R	TEAM
12.07.	WEST GERMANY	5:0	SWITZERLAND
13.07.	ARGENTINA	2:1	SPAIN
15.07.	SPAIN	2:1	SWITZERLAND
16.07.	WEST GERMANY	0:0	ARGENTINA
19.07.	ARGENTINA	2:0	SWITZERLAND
20.07.	WEST GERMANY	2:1	SPAIN

PTS: W. GERMANY 5, ARGENTINA 5, SPAIN 2, SWITZERLAND 0

GROUP 3

DATE	TEAM	R	TEAM
12.07.	BRAZIL	2:0	BULGARIA
13.07.	PORTUGAL	3:1	HUNGARY
15.07.	HUNGARY	3:1	BRAZIL
16.07.	PORTUGAL	3:0	BULGARIA
19.07.	PORTUGAL	3:1	BRAZIL
20.07.	HUNGARY	3:1	BULGARIA

PTS: PORTUGAL 6, HUNGARY 4, BRAZIL 2, BULGARIA 0

GROUP 4

DATE	TEAM	R	TEAM
12.07.	USSR	3:0	NORTH KOREA
13.07.	ITALY	2:0	CHILE
15.07.	NORTH KOREA	1:1	CHILE
16.07.	USSR	1:0	ITALY
19.07.	NORTH KOREA	1:0	ITALY
20.07.	USSR	2:1	CHILE

PTS: USSR 6, NORTH KOREA 3, ITALY 2, CHILE 1

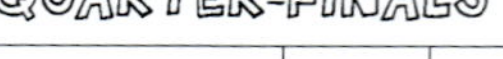

QUARTER-FINALS

DATE	TEAM	R	TEAM
23.07.	ENGLAND	1:0	ARGENTINA
23.07.	W. GERMANY	4:0	URUGUAY
23.07.	USSR	2:1	HUNGARY
23.07.	PORTUGAL	5:3	NORTH KOREA

SEMIFINALS

DATE	TEAM	R	TEAM
25.07.	W. GERMANY	2:1	USSR
26.07.	ENGLAND	2:1	PORTUGAL

3RD PLACE

DATE	TEAM	R	TEAM
28.07.	PORTUGAL	2:1	USSR

FINAL

DATE	TEAM	R	TEAM
30.07.	ENGLAND	4:2	W. GERMANY

TICKET FOR THE LEGENDARY WEMBLEY STADIUM 1966

THE QUEEN HANDS OVER THE TROPHY TO CAPTAIN BOBBY MOORE

CHAMPION: ENGLAND

QUALIFIED TEAMS
16 (FROM 71 CANDIDATES)

ATTENDANCE
1,563,135 (Ø: 48,848 PER MATCH)

PERIOD
11TH JULY, 1966–30TH JULY, 1966

PLAYERS IN FIELD
253

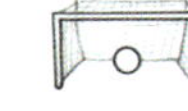

GOALS
89 (Ø: 2.78 PER MATCH)

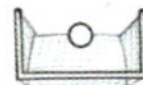

OWN GOALS
2

FASTEST GOAL
55 SECONDS: PAK SEUNG-ZIN (NORTH KOREA–PORTUGAL)

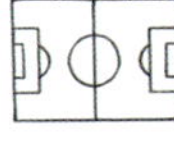

MATCHES
32

MOST DANGEROUS TEAM
PORTUGAL: 17 GOALS IN 6 MATCHES

TOP SCORERS
9 GOALS: EUSEBIO (PORTUGAL)
6 GOALS: HALLER (WEST GERMANY)
4 GOALS: HURST (ENGLAND), BECKENBAUER (WEST GERMANY), PORKUJAN (USSR), BENE (HUNGARY)

EXPULSIONS
5 (Ø: 0.16 PER MATCH)

BEST PLAYER TOP 3
1. BOBBY CHARLTON (ENGLAND)
2. EUSEBIO (PORTUGAL)
3. BOBBY MOORE (ENGLAND)

BEST GOALKEEPER
GORDON BANKS (ENGLAND)

3 OR MORE GOALS IN A MATCH
4 GOALS: EUSEBIO (PORTUGAL–NORTH KOREA)
3 GOALS: HURST (ENGLAND–WEST GERMANY)

PENALTIES
8: ALL SCORED

BEST YOUNG PLAYER
FRANZ BECKENBAUER, 20 YEARS (WEST GERMANY)

DREAM TEAM 1966

ACZEL

1970 MEXICO

PELÉ CELEBRATES HIS FIRST GOAL AGAINST ITALY. JAIRZINHO HOISTS HIM

1970 MEXICO

Mexico World Cup (May 31 to June 21) included three of the matches which are considered the best in the history of soccer. Yellow and red cards were used for the first time and the possibility to replace players by substitutes during the course of the game was introduced then. To the delight of the spectators, all matches were broadcast on color TV.

Most of the games were played in the middle of the day to suit European television and timetables, making heat a great threat for players' health. But despite that concern, some matches were wonderfully played and made history.

Pelé, who had decided not to play again in a World Cup after Brazil's early elimination in 1966, changed his mind and returned, in part, due to the pressure of the government. During the first stage, Brazil faced England, the last Champions, in a historic match, in which the English goalkeeper Gordon Banks, played brilliantly. He blocked Pelé´s header, threw the ball out and saved his team. But it was not enough. Jaizinho´s goal turned the result into 1-0 for Brazil.

The match between England and Germany in the quarter-finals (both finalists in 1966) was dramatic: with 20 minutes remaining, Germany was on the back foot, but Beckenbauer scored first, and Seeler equalized, and, in the extra time, 'the bomber' Müller, scored the last goal, turning the result into 3-2 for Germany. He had also scored successive hat-tricks against Bulgaria and Peru.

The Semifinal between Germany and Italy became the game of the century. Once again, Müller helped his team in the extra time, scoring twice. Italy was winning but 'the bomber' managed to equalize in the 110th minute. Neither his intervention nor Beckenbauer heroically playing with a dislocated shoulder and immobilized arm could prevent the defeat (3-4).

In the Final match against Brazil, 'La Squadra Azzurra' had their energies at low level. It was Pelé who opened the scoring and took part in two other goals. After the final outcome 4-1, Brazil took home the Cup for the third time. It was the last World Cup for Pelé, who retired with glory.

PELÉ AND BOBBY MOORE SWAP SHIRTS AFTER BRAZIL'S EPIC VICTORY 1–0

THE PERFECT TACKLE: BOBBY MOORE STOPS JAIRZINHO WITH A TACKLE THAT SILENCED THE SPECTATORS...

...BUT HE WHO LAUGHS LAST, LAUGHS BEST. JAIRZINHO SCORES THE VICTORY GOAL AGAINST ENGLAND

THE SAVE BY GORDON BANKS FROM ENGLAND IS CONSIDERED THE BEST IN WORLD CUP HISTORY. BANKS MANAGED TO PALM THE BALL COMING FROM PELÉ'S HEADER THAT WAS DESTINED FOR THE BOTTOM CORNER

TOP SCORER (TEN GOALS) GERD MÜLLER WEST GERMANY BEATS ENGLISH STAND-IN GOALKEEPER PETER BONETTI, KNOCKING THE REIGNING CHAMPION OUT IN THE QUARTER-FINAL

1970 WORLD CUP WAS THE FIRST TO BE TELEVISED IN COLOR

THE EMPEROR

FRANZ BECKENBAUER CONTINUED PLAYING DURING THE SEMIFINAL AGAINST ITALY, DESPITE HAVING DISLOCATED HIS SHOULDER. ITALY WON IN EXTRA TIME 4-3, BUT THE REAL WINNER WAS SOCCER!

UUUUUH!!! PELÉ SHOOTS FROM HIS OWN HALF IN THE MATCH AGAINST CZECHOSLOVAQUIA, BUT THE BALL PASSES REALLY CLOSE TO THE GOAL POST

ANOTHER GOAL THAT WAS NOT POSSIBLE: PELÉ , FOOLS MAZURKIEWICZ, URUGUAYAN GOALKEEPER, WITH A DUMMY WITHOUT TOUCHING THE BALL, FEINTS, LEAVES IT. THE GOALKEEPER ALONE, NO PLAYER, NO BALL. PELÉ TURNS, RETRIEVES THE BALL AGAIN BUT SHOOTS WIDE... AMAZING!!!

A SOCCER LESSON: HOW TO STOP THE BALL WITH THE CHEST. PELÉ AND HIS GOAL AGAINST CZECHOSLOVAKIA

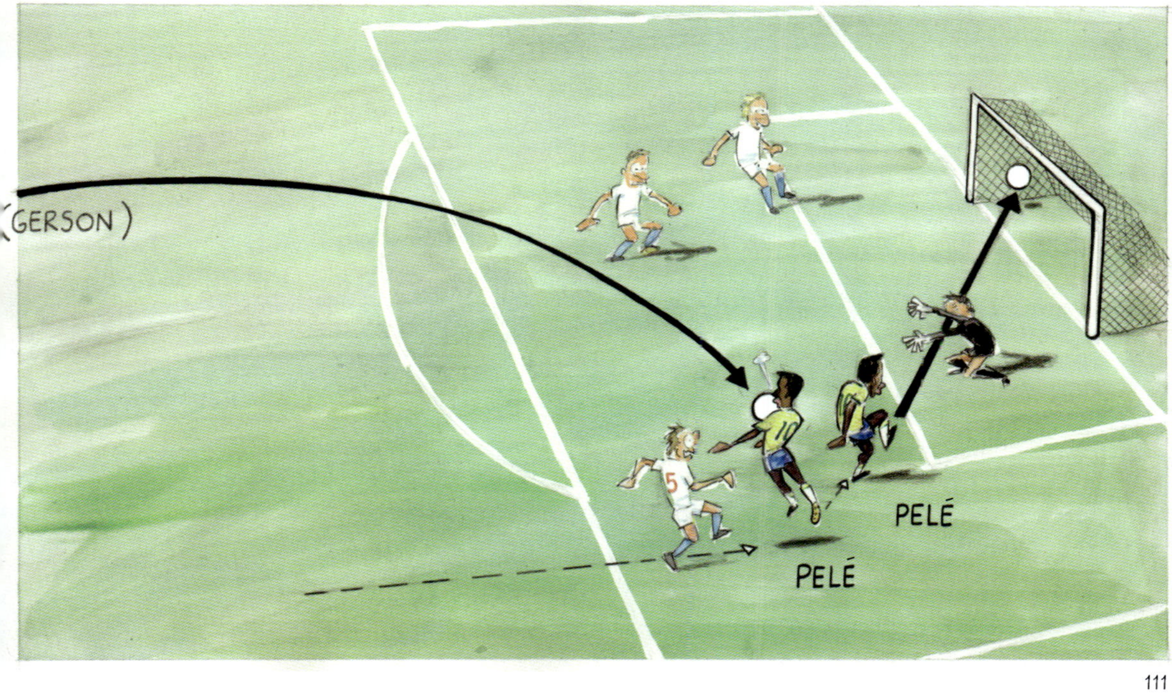

(GERSON)

PELÉ

PELÉ

1970 WORLD CHAMPIONS: BRAZIL.
CARLOS ALBERTO, BRITO, GERSON, PIAZZA, EVERALDO,
TOSTÃO, CLODOALDO, RIVELINO, PELÉ, JAIRZINHO, FÉLIX

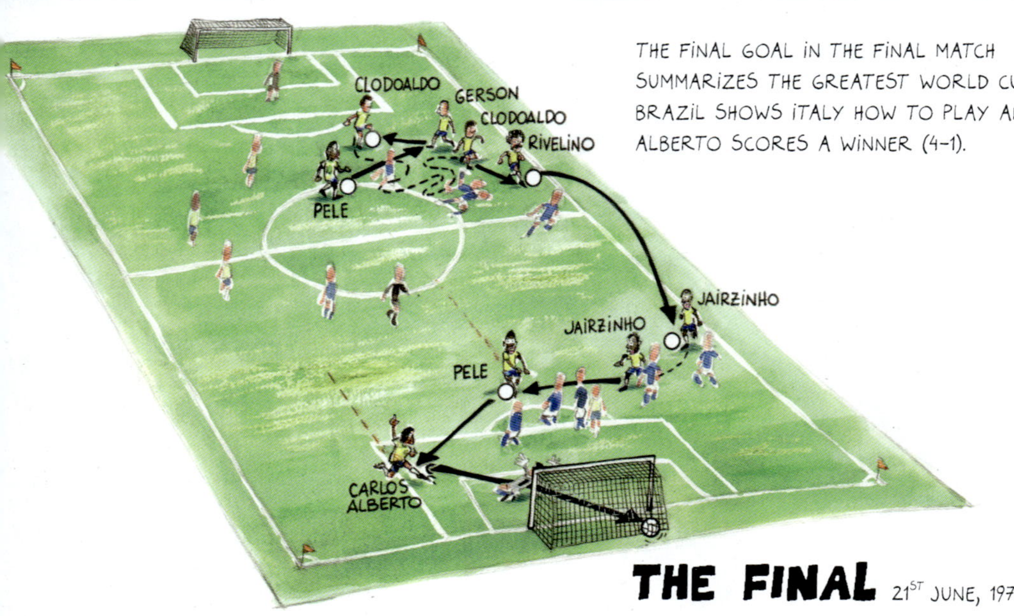

THE FINAL GOAL IN THE FINAL MATCH SUMMARIZES THE GREATEST WORLD CUP OF ALL. BRAZIL SHOWS ITALY HOW TO PLAY AND CARLOS ALBERTO SCORES A WINNER (4-1).

THE FINAL 21ST JUNE, 1970

BRAZIL 4:1 ITALY

ESTADIO AZTECA, MÉXICO CITY
ATTENDANCE: 107,412
REFEREE: RUDI GLÖCKNER (EAST GERMANY)

MÁRIO ZAGALLO WAS THE FIRST MAN TO WIN THE WORLD CUP AS A PLAYER IN 1958 AND 1962 AND LATER AS A COACH IN 1970

18TH MINUTE
1:0 PELÉ HEADER
1:1 BONINSEGNA
37TH MINUTE
2:1 GERSON FROM 17 METRES
66TH MINUTE
3:1 JAIRZINHO
72ND MINUTE
4:1 CARLOS ALBERTO. THE BEST GOAL OF THE CUP
87TH MINUTE
BRAZIL ARE THE WORLD CUP WINNERS AND PELÉ BECOMES THE KING OF SOCCER
Pelé
ACZEL

1970 IN OVERVIEW

GROUP 1

DATE	TEAM	R	TEAM
31.05.	MEXICO	0:0	USSR
03.06.	BELGIUM	3:0	EL SALVADOR
06.06.	USSR	4:1	BELGIUM
07.06.	MEXICO	4:0	EL SALVADOR
10.06.	USSR	2:0	EL SALVADOR
11.06.	MEXICO	1:0	BELGIUM

PTS: USSR 5, MEXICO 5, BELGIUM 2, EL SALVADOR 0

GROUP 2

DATE	TEAM	R	TEAM
02.06.	URUGUAY	2:0	ISRAEL
03.06.	ITALY	1:0	SWEDEN
06.06.	URUGUAY	0:0	ITALY
07.06.	SWEDEN	1:1	ISRAEL
10.06.	SWEDEN	1:0	URUGUAY
11.06.	ITALY	0:0	ISRAEL

PTS: ITALY 4, URUGUAY 3, SWEDEN 3, ISRAEL 2

GROUP 3

DATE	TEAM	R	TEAM
02.06.	ENGLAND	1:0	ROMANIA
03.06.	BRAZIL	4:1	CZECHOSLOVAKIA
06.06.	ROMANIA	2:1	CZECHOSLOVAKIA
07.06.	BRAZIL	1:0	ENGLAND
10.06.	BRAZIL	3:2	ROMANIA
11.06.	ENGLAND	1:0	CZECHOSLOVAKIA

PTS: BRAZIL 6, ENGLAND 4, ROMANIA 2, CZECHOSLOVAKIA 0

GROUP 4

DATE	TEAM	R	TEAM
02.06.	PERU	3:2	BULGARIA
03.06.	WEST GERMANY	2:1	MOROCCO
06.06.	PERU	3:0	MOROCCO
07.06.	WEST GERMANY	5:2	BULGARIA
10.06.	WEST GERMANY	3:1	PERU
11.06.	BULGARIA	1:1	MOROCCO

PTS: WEST GERMANY 6, PERU 4, BULGARIA 1, MOROCCO 1

QUARTER-FINALS

DATE	TEAM	R	TEAM
14.06.	BRAZIL	4:2	PERU
14.06.	W. GERMANY	3:2	ENGLAND
14.06.	ITALY	4:1	MEXICO
14.06.	URUGUAY	1:0	USSR

SEMIFINALS

DATE	TEAM	R	TEAM
17.06.	BRAZIL	3:1	URUGUAY
17.06.	ITALY	4:3	W. GERMANY

3RD PLACE

DATE	TEAM	R	TEAM
20.06.	W. GERMANY	1:0	URUGUAY

FINAL

DATE	TEAM	R	TEAM
21.06.	BRAZIL	4:1	ITALY

TICKET 1970

BRAZIL COULD KEEP THE GOLDEN TROPHY AFTER THREE WINS OF THE WORLD CUP. UNFORTUNATELY, IT WAS STOLEN AND NEVER APPEARED AGAIN

CHAMPION:
BRAZIL

QUALIFIED TEAMS

16 (FROM 70 CANDIDATES)

PERIOD

31TH MAY, 1970–21TH JUNE, 1970

ATTENDANCE

1,603,975 (Ø: 50,124 PER MATCH)

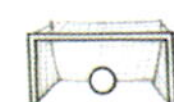

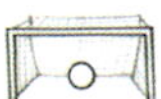

GOALS

95 (Ø: 2.97 PER MATCH)

PLAYERS IN FIELD

275

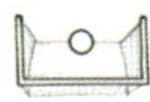

OWN GOALS

0

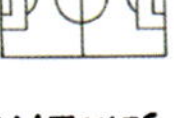

MATCHES

32

FASTEST GOAL

4 MINUTES: PETRAS (CZECHOSLOVAKIA–ROMANIA)

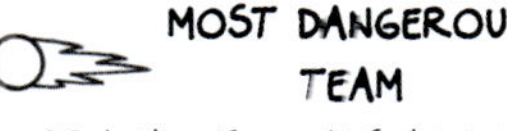

MOST DANGEROUS TEAM

BRAZIL: 19 GOALS IN 6 MATCHES

TOP SCORERS

10 GOALS: MÜLLER (WEST GERMANY

7 GOALS: JAIRZINHO (BRAZIL)

5 GOALS: CUBILLAS (PERU)

FAIR PLAY AWARD

PERU

BEST PLAYER TOP 3

1. PELÉ (BRAZIL)
2. GERD MÜLLER (WEST GERMANY)
3. JAIRZINHO (BRAZIL)

YELLOW CARDS

33 (Ø: 1.03 PER MATCH)

RED CARDS

0

BEST GOALKEEPER

LADISLAO MAZURKIEWICZ (URUGUAY)

3 OR MORE GOALS IN A MATCH

3 GOALS: MÜLLER (WEST GERMANY–BULGARIA), MÜLLER (WEST GERMANY–PERU)

PENALTIES

5: ALL SCORED

BEST YOUNG PLAYER

TEÓFILO CUBILLAS, 21 YEARS (PERU)

DREAM TEAM 1970

17

1974 WEST GERMANY

GERD MÜLLER'S GOAL IN THE FINAL WAS THE MOST IMPORTANT OF MANY HE SCORED IN HIS CAREER

AS BRAZIL KEPT THE JULES RIMET TROPHY AFTER WINNING IT FOR THE THIRD TIME, A NEW CUP WAS INTRODUCED IN 1974

1974 WEST GERMANY

'Emperor against King', East against West, a new cup and the first World Cup with penalties was introduced. The tournament that took place in West Germany (June 13 to July 7) was full of news. For the first time, a new super-team was ready to take over the world with their characteristic orange shirt: it was Netherlands.

Jürgen Sparwasser was right when he said, "Everybody would know who was buried under the gravestone with the inscription: Hamburg, 1974." Sparwasser, forward from East Germany referred to the moment when he scored his famous goal in Hansestadt against West Germany in the group stage and won the match (1-0).

The Dutch national team was first in their group. Despite this being only their third World Cup (1934 and 1938), the 'Orange' made clear that, after four victories in the Champions League, they would be part of international soccer. Seven players were part of Feyenoord Rotterdam, and six were from Ajax of Amsterdam. Both teams had been on a winning streak in Europe. However, the star of the Cup was Johan Cruyff, 'the King of Europe', who was awarded in 1999 the title 'Best European Player of the 20th Century'.

The German team was also legendary. Five of their players played for Borussia Mönchengladbach and seven for FC Bayern including Vogts, Heynckes, Maier, Breitner, Beckenbauer and Müller. West Germany National Team marched to the final and faced an equally dominating Netherlands. The first goal in the final came just two minutes after kick-off, following a penalty converted by Johan Neeskens, making it the fastest goal ever scored in a World Cup final. Breitner equalized with a penalty as well, and 18 minutes later, Müller's goal made it 2–1, giving Germany the lead they held until the final whistle. Franz Beckenbauer, or 'the Emperor' beat the 'king' Johan Cruyff. The champions received a sum of 60,000 Marks and a Volkswagen for each player; this time the prizes were even better than in 1954.

FRANZ BECKENBAUER HOLDS THE NEW CUP, A SOLID GOLD TROPHY THAT SYMBOLIZED THE START OF A NEW ERA

GERMANY FACED POLAND IN THE SECOND GROUP STAGE UNDER A HEAVY RAIN THAT SATURATED THE PITCH

OOPS!...JUST A MOMENT BEFORE THE FINAL, OFFICIALS REALIZED THERE WAS SOMETHING MISSING...

GRZEGORZ LATO FROM POLAND, WON THE GOLDEN BOOT WITH SEVEN GOALS

MWEPU, A PLAYER FROM ZAIRE, RAN OUT OF THE DEFENSIVE WALL TO HAMMER THE BALL BEFORE BRAZIL COULD TAKE THE FREE KICK

1974 WORLD CUP'S ORIGINAL HAIRSTYLES

THE MAJESTIC JOHAN CRUYFF WAS DEFINITELY THE BEST PLAYER OF 1974 WORLD CUP, BUT HE COULD NEVER GAIN VICTORY IN A WORLD CUP
14

ARGENTINA WAS BLOWN AWAY BY THE DUTCH IN THE SECOND GROUP STAGE 4-0. THE SECOND GOAL WAS A CLASSIC OF CRUYFF

THE CRUYFF TURN

CRUYFF'S BRILLIANT VOLEY IN THE SEMIFINAL AGANST BRAZIL

1974 WORLD CHAMPIONS: WEST GERMANY.
FRANZ BECKENBAUER, SEPP MAYER, HANS-GEORG SCHWARZENBECK, RAINER BONHOF, BERND HÖLZENBEIN, JÜRGEN GRABOWSKI, GERD MÜLLER, WOLFGANG OVERATH, BERTI VOGTS, PAUL BREITNER, ULI HOENESS

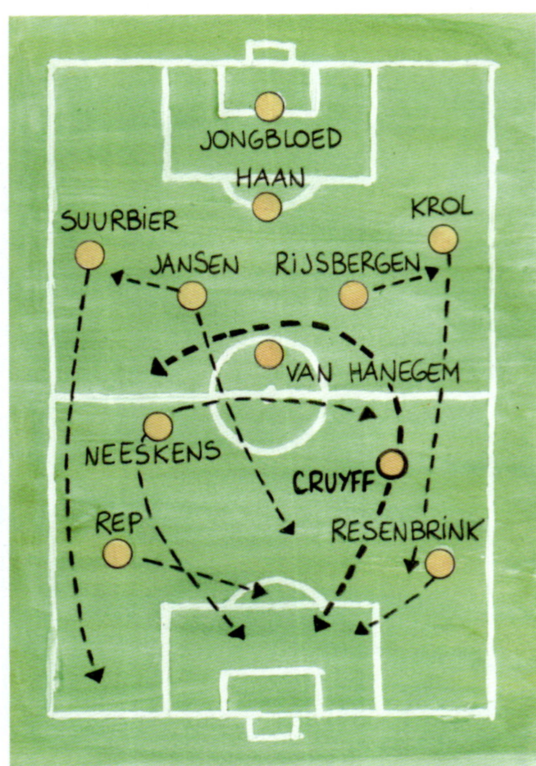

(LEFT) NETHERLANDS 'A CLOCKWORK ORANGE' AND THEIR 'TOTAL SOCCER' WHICH MEANT THAT EVERY PLAYER COULD PLAY EVERYWHERE

(RIGHT) GERD MÜLLER CELEBRATES HIS WIN IN THE FINAL. THE LAST OF 68 GOALS SCORED IN A TOTAL OF 62 INTERNATIONAL MATCHES

THE FINAL 7TH JULY, 1974

WEST GERMANY 2:1 NETHERLANDS

OLYMPIA STADIUM, MÜNCHEN
ATTENDANCE: 75,200
REFEREE: JACK TAYLOR (ENGLAND)

WEST GERMANY COACH, 'DER LANGE' HELMUT SCHÖN

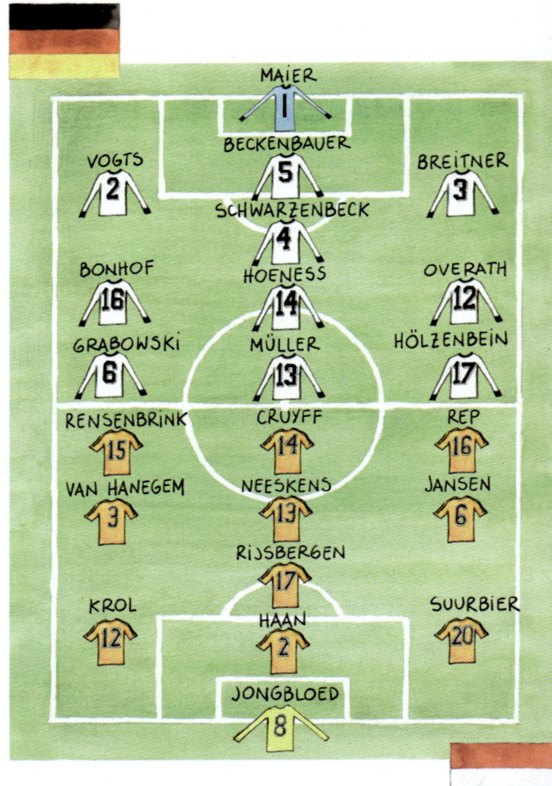

TWO LEGENDS SHAKE HANDS: FRANZ BECKENBAUER AND JOHAN CRUYFF BEFORE THE FINAL
1ST MINUTE
HOENESS FOULS CRUYFF: PENALTY!!!
0:1 JOHAN NEESKENS
25TH MINUTE
HOLZENBEIN FOULED: PENALTY!!!
1:1 PAUL BREITNER
2:1
'DER BOMBER' TURNS AND SHOOTS, SCORING THE WINNING GOAL
44TH MINUTE
WEST GERMANY WORLD CHAMPION!

1974 IN OVERVIEW

GROUP I

DATE	TEAM	R	TEAM
14.06.	WEST GERMANY	1:0	CHILE
14.06.	EAST GERMANY	2:0	AUSTRALIA
18.06.	AUSTRALIA	0:3	WEST GERMANY
18.06.	CHILE	1:1	EAST GERMANY
22.06.	AUSTRALIA	0:0	CHILE
22.06.	EAST GERMANY	1:0	WEST GERMANY

PTS: E. GERMANY 5, W. GERMANY 4, CHILE 2, AUSTRALIA 1

GROUP II

DATE	TEAM	R	TEAM
13.06.	BRAZIL	0:0	YUGOSLAVIA
14.06.	ZAIRE	0:2	SCOTLAND
18.06.	SCOTLAND	0:0	BRAZIL
18.06.	YUGOSLAVIA	9:0	ZAIRE
22.06.	SCOTLAND	1:1	YUGOSLAVIA
22.06.	ZAIRE	0:3	BRAZIL

PTS: YUGOSLAVIA 4, BRAZIL 4, SCOTLAND 4, ZAIRE 0

GROUP III

DATE	TEAM	R	TEAM
15.06.	SWEDEN	0:0	BULGARIA
15.06.	URUGUAY	0:2	NETHERLANDS
19.06.	NETHERLANDS	0:0	SWEDEN
19.06.	BULGARIA	1:1	URUGUAY
23.06.	BULGARIA	1:4	NETHERLANDS
23.06.	SWEDEN	3:0	URUGUAY

PTS: NETHERLANDS 5, SWEDEN 4, BULGARIA 2, URUGUAY 1

GROUP IV

DATE	TEAM	R	TEAM
15.06.	ITALY	3:1	HAITI
15.06.	POLAND	3:2	ARGENTINA
19.06.	ARGENTINA	1:1	ITALY
19.06.	HAITI	0:7	POLAND
23.06.	POLAND	2:1	ITALY
23.06.	ARGENTINA	4:1	HAITI

PTS: POLAND 6, ARGENTINA 3, ITALY 3, HAITI 0

SECOND ROUND

GROUP A

DATE	TEAM	R	TEAM
26.06.	NETHERLANDS	4:0	ARGENTINA
26.06.	BRAZIL	1:0	E. GERMANY
30.06.	ARGENTINA	1:2	BRAZIL
30.06.	E. GERMANY	0:2	NETHERLANDS
03.07.	ARGENTINA	1:1	E. GERMANY
03.07.	NETHERLANDS	2:0	BRAZIL

PTS: NETHERLANDS 6, BRAZIL 4, E. GERMANY 1, ARGENTINA 1

GROUP B

DATE	TEAM	R	TEAM
26.06.	YUGOSLAVIA	0:2	W. GERMANY
26.06.	SWEDEN	0:1	POLAND
30.06.	POLAND	2:1	YUGOSLAVIA
30.06.	W. GERMANY	4:2	SWEDEN
03.07.	POLAND	0:1	W. GERMANY
03.07.	SWEDEN	2:1	YUGOSLAVIA

PTS: WEST GERMANY 6, POLAND 4, SWEDEN 2, YUGOSLAVIA 0

3RD PLACE

DATE	TEAM	R	TEAM
06.07.	BRAZIL	0:1	POLAND

FINAL

DATE	TEAM	R	TEAM
07.07.	NETHERLANDS	1:2	W. GERMANY

CHAMPION: WEST GERMANY

TICKET 1974

WEST GERMANY BUS

QUALIFIED TEAMS
16 (FROM 99 CANDIDATES)

PERIOD
13TH JUNE, 1974–07TH JULY, 1974

ATTENDANCE
1,865,753 (Ø: 49,099 PER MATCH)

GOALS
97 (Ø: 2.55 PER MATCH)

OWN GOALS
4

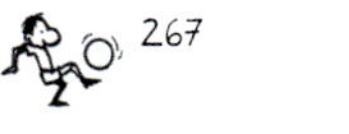

PLAYERS IN FIELD
267

FASTEST GOAL
80 SECONDS: NEESKENS
(NETHERLANDS–WEST GERMANY)

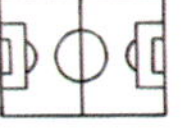

MATCHES
38

TORGEFÄHRLICHSTE MANNSCHAFT
POLAND: 16 GOALS IN 7 MATCHES

TOP SCORERS
7 GOALS: LATO (POLAND)
5 GOALS: SZARMACH (POLAND),
NEESKENS (NETHERLANDS)

FAIR PLAY AWARD
WEST GERMANY

BEST PLAYER TOP 3
1. JOHAN CRUYFF (NETHERLANDS)
2. FRANZ BECKENBAUER (WEST GERMANY)
3. GRZEGORZ LATO (POLAND), JOHAN NEESKENS (NETHERLANDS)

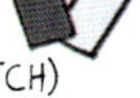

YELLOW CARDS
87 (Ø: 2.29 PER MATCH)

RED CARDS
5 (Ø: 0.13 PER MATCH)

BEST GOALKEEPER
SEPP MAYER (WEST GERMANY)

3 OR MORE GOALS IN A MATCH
3 GOALS: BAJEVI (YUGOSLAVIA–ZAIRE)
SZARMACH (POLAND–HAITI)

PENALTIES
8: 6 SCORED,
2 SAVED

BEST YOUNG PLAYER
WADYSAW MUDA,
20 YEARS (POLAND)

DREAM TEAM 1974

1978 ARGENTINA

THE PAPER STORM. ONE OF THE MOST BEAUTIFUL IMAGES OF 1978 WORLD CUP

1978 ARGENTINA

The XI World Cup took place in Argentina from June 1 to 25, 1978, in 6 stadiums in the cities of Buenos Aires, Rosario, Mar del Plata, Córdoba, and Mendoza. Thus, the Cup returned to South America after 16 years.

The official ball underwent a revolutionary change with the appearance of the new Adidas Tango. This ball, with better water resistance, became a classic design that lasted five World Cups. It was said that Cruyff, as well as other glorious players of 1974, did not want to participate in Argentina's Cup due to the dictatorship governing the country. The Dutch committed themselves not to receive the Cup in case they won.

The German National Team, holders of the Cup, arrived in Argentina confident in their chances. There was a hit that was broadcast on German radio: a song by Udo Jürgens, "Buenos días Argentina," which the German team lively chanted. However, they drew two games 0-0 against Poland and Tunisia. After two more draws in the second round, Germany had to beat Austria, who had already been eliminated, but Austria's 3-2 win sent the reigning champions home. The match was later called 'the humiliation of Córdoba'. On the other hand, the Netherlands reached the final after an amazing long shot by Arie Haan.

In order to proceed to the final, Argentina had to beat Peru with a four-goal difference at least, as Brazil had a better goal difference. In fact, the match ended 6-0, and rumors of political and military pressure circulated ever since. Additionally, Peru's goalkeeper, who was born in Argentina, had a terrible game.

Mario Kempes, called 'el matador', justified his nickname by scoring twice in the final and playing a significant role in winning soccer's ultimate prize. Four years later, Kempes gave his number 10 shirt to Maradona, the superstar who would later on hold the World Cup for his country.

MARIO KEMPES, CALLED 'EL MATADOR', CELEBRATES HIS GOAL AGAINST THE NETHERLANDS IN THE FINAL AND GALVANISES THE WHOLE OF ARGENTINA. HE WON THE GOLDEN BOOT WITH SIX GOALS

ARCHIE GEMMILL

ARCHIE GEMMILL'S GOAL FOR SCOTLAND IN THE MATCH AGAINST NETHERLANDS WAS A SPARK OF GLORY!

WORLD CUP GOAL NUMBER 1000

THE PENALTY SCORED BY DUTCH ROB RENSENBRINK IN THE MATCH AGAINST SCOTLAND WAS THE GOAL NUMBER 1000

CLIVE THOMAS REFEREE FROM WALES, TOOK SOCCER RULES TOO SERIOUSLY. DURING BRAZIL'S MATCH AGAINST SWEDEN, HE RULED OUT A GOAL FROM ZICO, WHICH WOULD HAVE HELP THEM TO WIN THE MATCH, SAYING HE HAD BLOWN FOR FULL TIME WHEN THE BALL WAS IN THE AIR FOLLOWING A CORNER

WHEN FRANCE FACED HUNGARY, THEIR KITS LOOKED SIMILAR ON ARGENTINA'S BLACK AND WHITE TELEVISION SYSTEM. SO FRANCE WORE SHIRTS BORROWED FROM ATLÉTICO KIMBERLEY, A CLUB FROM MAR DEL PLATA

17-YEAR-OLD MARADONA WAS REALLY UPSET BECAUSE CESAR LUIS MENOTTI, ARGENTINA'S COACH, HAD LEFT HIM OUT OF THE FINAL SQUAD OF 22 PLAYERS

ARIE HAAN, FROM THE NETHERLANDS, SCORED WITH A SHOT FROM DISTANCE THAT SURPRISED DINO ZOFF AND PUT HIS TEAM INTO THE FINAL INSTEAD OF ITALY

ZOFF WAS BEATEN AGAIN... ...THIS TIME DUE TO NELINHO'S FABULOUS CURVING SHOT THAT WON BRAZIL THE THIRD PLACE PLAY-OFF

DANIEL PASSARELLA, CAPTAIN OF ARGENTINA'S TEAM, HOLDS THE CUP ALOFT AS THE WHOLE NATION SHARES A JOY LIKE NO OTHER!

ARGENT
78
AFA

1978 WORLD CHAMPIONS: ARGENTINA.
TOP: DANIEL PASSARELLA, DANIEL BERTONI, JORGE OLGUÍN, ALBERTO TARANTINI,
MARIO KEMPES, UBALDO FILLOL. BOTTOM: AMÉRICO GALLEGO, OSVALDO ARDÍLES
LEOPOLDO LUQUE, OSCAR ORTIZ, LUIS GALVÁN.

ARGENTINA NEEDED TO SCORE FOUR GOALS IN THE MATCH AGAINST PERU TO GET TO THE FINAL AND SCORED SIX. BUT EVERYONE NOTICED THAT PERU'S GOALKEEPER WAS ARGENTINIAN, BORN IN ROSARIO, THE CITY WHERE THE MATCH TOOK PLACE

ARGENTINA 6:0 PERU

'EL FLACO' MENOTTI (THE SKINNY ONE), ARGENTINA'S COACH AND CHAIN SMOKER, MIXED SOUTH AMERICAN FLAIR AND EUROPEAN DISCIPLINE IN HIS TACTICS

THE FINAL 25TH JUNE, 1978

ARGENTINA 3:1 NETHERLANDS (EXTRA-TIME)

ESTADIO MONUMENTAL, BUENOS AIRES

ATTENDANCE: 71,483

REFEREE: SERGIO GONELLA (ITALY)

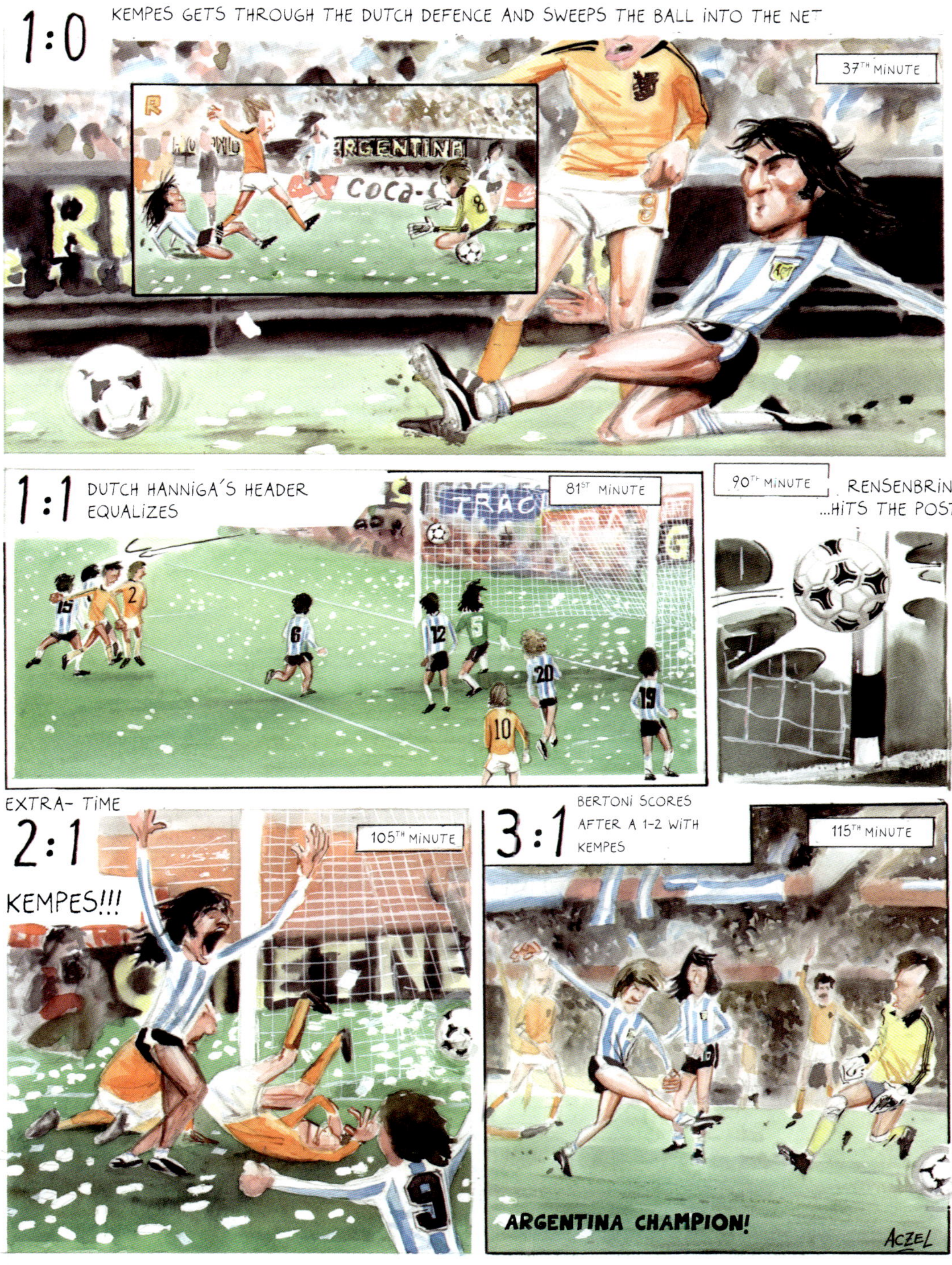

1:0
KEMPES GETS THROUGH THE DUTCH DEFENCE AND SWEEPS THE BALL INTO THE NET
37TH MINUTE

1:1
DUTCH HANNIGA´S HEADER EQUALIZES
81ST MINUTE

90TH MINUTE
RENSENBRINK...
...HITS THE POST!!!

1978 IN OVERVIEW

GROUP 1

DATE	TEAM	R	TEAM
02.06.	ITALY	2:1	FRANCE
02.06.	ARGENTINA	2:1	HUNGARY
06.06.	ITALY	3:1	HUNGARY
06.06.	ARGENTINA	2:1	FRANCE
10.06.	FRANCE	3:1	HUNGARY
10.06.	ITALY	1:0	ARGENTINA

PTS: ITALY 6, ARGENTINA 4, FRANCE 2, HUNGARY 0

GROUP 2

DATE	TEAM	R	TEAM
01.06.	WEST GERMANY	0:0	POLAND
02.06.	TUNISIA	3:1	MEXICO
06.06.	POLAND	1:0	TUNISIA
06.06.	WEST GERMANY	6:0	MEXICO
10.06.	WEST GERMANY	0:0	TUNISIA
10.06.	POLAND	3:1	MEXICO

PTS: POLAND 5, WEST GERMANY 4, TUNISIA 3, MEXICO 0

GROUP 3

DATE	TEAM	R	TEAM
03.06.	SWEDEN	1:1	BRAZIL
03.06.	AUSTRIA	2:1	SPAIN
07.06.	AUSTRIA	1:0	SWEDEN
07.06.	BRAZIL	0:0	SPAIN
11.06.	BRAZIL	1:0	AUSTRIA
11.06.	SPAIN	1:0	SWEDEN

PTS: AUSTRIA 4, BRAZIL 4, SPAIN 3, SWEDEN 1

GROUP 4

DATE	TEAM	R	TEAM
03.06.	NETHERLANDS	3:0	IRAN
03.06.	PERU	3:1	SCOTLAND
07.06.	SCOTLAND	1:1	IRAN
07.06.	NETHERLANDS	0:0	PERU
11.06.	SCOTLAND	3:2	NETHERLANDS
11.06.	PERU	4:1	IRAN

PTS: PERU 5, NETHERLANDS 3, SCOTLAND 3, IRAN 1

SECOND ROUND

GROUP A

DATE	TEAM	R	TEAM
14.06.	W. GERMANY	0:0	ITALY
14.06.	NETHERLANDS	5:1	AUSTRIA
18.06.	ITALY	1:0	AUSTRIA
18.06.	W. GERMANY	2:2	NETHERLANDS
21.06.	NETHERLANDS	2:1	ITALY
21.06.	AUSTRIA	3:2	W. GERMANY

PTS: NETHERLANDS 5, ITALY 3, WEST GERMANY 2, AUSTRIA 2

GROUP B

DATE	TEAM	R	TEAM
14.06.	BRAZIL	3:0	PERU
14.06.	ARGENTINA	2:0	POLAND
18.06.	POLAND	1:0	PERU
18.06.	ARGENTINA	0:0	BRAZIL
21.06.	BRAZIL	3:1	POLAND
21.06.	ARGENTINA	6:0	PERU

PTS: ARGENTINA 5, BRAZIL 5, POLAND 2, PERU 0

3RD PLACE

DATE	TEAM	R	TEAM
24.06.	BRAZIL	2:1	ITALY

FINAL

DATE	TEAM	R	TEAM
25.06.	ARGENTINA	3:1 (E.T)	NETHERLANDS

CHAMPION: ARGENTINA

TICKET 1978

ELECTRONIC SCREEN AT ESTADIO MONUMENTAL: 'ARGENTINA CHAMPION!'

QUALIFIED TEAMS
16 (FROM 106 CANDIDATES)

PLAYERS IN FIELD

278

FASTEST GOAL
31 SECONDS: BERNARD LACOMBE (FRANCE–ITALY)

TOP SCORERS
6 GOALS: KEMPES (ARGENTINA)
5 GOALS: CUBILLAS (PERU), RENSENBRINK (NETHERLANDS)

BEST GOALKEEPER
UBALDO FILLOL (ARGENTINA)

BEST YOUNG PLAYER
ANTONIO CABRINI, 20 YEARS (ITALY)

PERIOD
1ST JUNE, 1978–25TH JUNE, 1978

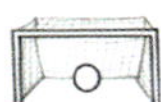

GOALS
102 (Ø: 2.68 PER MATCH)

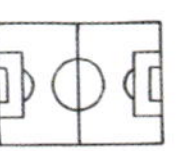

MATCHES
38

FAIR PLAY AWARD
ARGENTINA

YELLOW CARDS
58 (Ø: 1.53 PER MATCH)

RED CARDS
3 (Ø: 0.08 PER MATCH)

3 OR MORE GOALS IN A MATCH
3 GOALS: RENSENBRINK (INCLUDING 2 PENALTIES, NETHERLANDS–IRAN), CUBILLAS (INCLUDING 2 PENALTIES, PERU–IRAN)

ATTENDANCE
1,545,791 (Ø: 40,679 PER MATCH)

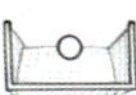

OWN GOALS
3

MOST DANGEROUS TEAM
ARGENTINA UND NETHERLANDS: BOTH 15 GOALS IN 7 MATCHES

BEST PLAYER TOP 3

1. MARIO KEMPES (ARGENTINA)
2. TEÓFILO CUBILLAS (PERU)
3. ROB RENSENBRINK (NETHERLANDS)

PENALTIES
14: 12 SCORED, 2 MISSED

DREAM TEAM 1978

GO

1982 SPAIN

MARCO TARDELLI, AFTER SCORING A GOAL IN THE FINAL AGAINST WEST GERMANY. HIS CELEBRATION WILL BE ALWAYS REMEMBERED AS THE GREATEST ONE

1982 SPAIN

The final of the Spain World Cup (June 13 to July 11) was played by two teams that had not played well during the first stage. An Italian forward, a very skinny player, created his own legend during the final stage.

This was the first time in which 24 teams qualified for the Cup. The Netherlands, runners up in 1974 and 1978, did not make it to the final stage.

German fans could not hide their displeasure at seeing their team lose 1-2 against Algeria in their opening match. But what was truly scandalous was their game against Austria: since a narrow Germany victory would be enough for both teams to advance, there was an unspoken "non-aggression pact" that made the match a tedious and dull display of soccer.

Hungary's 10–1 victory over El Salvador is still the most lopsided win in World Cup history. Argentina showed only a few flashes of Diego Armando Maradona's magic, as he was making his World Cup debut. The number 10 was fouled constantly, grew frustrated, and was sent off in the second stage against Brazil.

Brazil, the great favorite to win the title, needed only a draw against Italy to advance to the semifinals, but opted to play their "jogo bonito" instead of using a defensive approach. It was a huge mistake: Paolo Rossi made history by scoring a hat-trick that eliminated Brazil, sealing the match with a 3–2 final score.

In the intense West Germany vs. France semifinal, a dramatic moment unfolded when goalkeeper Harald Schumacher collided with Patrick Battiston, leaving him unconscious and forcing him to leave the field. The French were leading 3-1 in extra time until Karl-Heinz Rummenigge and Klaus Fischer brought the score level, and for the first time a shoot-out from the penalty spot decided the match, with the Germans emerging victorious.

Weakened after that grueling battle, West Germany faced a surprising Italy in the final, who won 3-1 thanks to a brace from Rossi and Tardelli, all scored in the second half. The Azzurri then hoisted the cup, bringing it back to European hands.

LIFE BEGINS AT 40! DINO ZOFF WAS PART OF THE CHAMPIONS TEAM; HE WAS 40 YEARS OLD! THIS GAVE HOPE TO MILLIONS OF MEN

SHEIK AL-AHMAD AL-SABAH, PRESIDENT OF KUWAITI FOOTBALL ASSOCIATION, GETS HIS TEAM OUT OF THE FIELD AFTER A DISPUTED GOAL SCORED BY FRANCE. THE REFEREE CHANGED HIS MIND

BELLOUMI'S GREAT GOAL HELPS ALGERIA TO A SHOCK 2-1 VICTORY IN THE MATCH AGAINST WEST GERMANY IN GROUP 2

THE GERMANS WENT THROUGH TO THE NEXT ROUN AFTER A MEANINGLESS ENCOUNTER IN WHICH BOT TEAMS AGREED NOT TO ATTACK EACH OTHER, A AUSTRIA HAD ALREADY QUALIFIED AND GERMAN ONLY NEEDED A VICTORY OF 1-

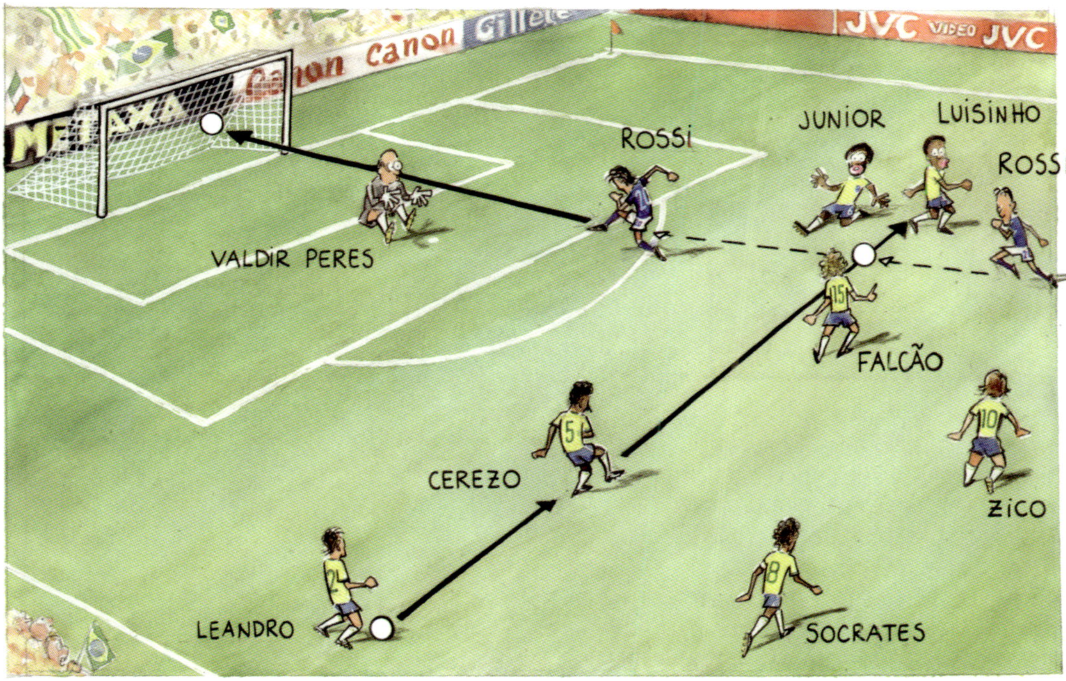

BRAZIL WERE FAVORITES, BUT THEIR WEAK DEFENDING LET THEM DOWN. CEREZO PASSES THE BALL AND PAOLO ROSSI SCORES THE SECOND OF HIS HAT-TRICK. ITALY WON 3-2

PAOLO ROSSI, (BEST GOAL SCORER WITH 6 GOALS) AFTER HAVING BEEN CRITICIZED IN THE FIRST STAGE, CAME BACK STRONGER AND PUT BRAZIL THE BEST TEAM (UP TO THEN) OUT OF THE TOURNAMENT

IN THE SEMIFINAL GERMAN GOALKEEPER HARALD SCHUMACHER KNOCKED DOWN PATRICK BATTISTON FROM FRANCE TO STOP A GOAL-SCORING OPPORTUNITY. DUE TO THE BRUTAL FOUL, THE FRENCH HAD TO BE ADMINISTERED OXYGEN AND PLATINI THOUGHT HE WAS DEAD. SCHUMACHER ON BEING TOLD BATTISTON HAD LOST THREE TEETH SAID, "IF ALL THAT'S WRONG WITH HIM, I'LL BUY HIM THE CROWNS." ALL THE DUTCH REFEREE DID WAS GIVE A GOALKICK!

ACZEL

1982 WORLD CHAMPIONS: ITALY.
TOP: DINO ZOFF, FRANCESCO GRAZIANI, GIUSEPPE BERGOMI, GAETANO SCIREA, FULVIO COLLOVATI, CLAUDIO GENTILE. BOTTOM: BRUNO CONTI, PAOLO ROSSI, GABRIELE ORIALI, ANTONIO CABRINI, MARCO TARDELLI.

MICHEL PLATINI, FRENCH CAPTAIN, WAS AN EXCEPTIONAL PLAYER. BUT HIS HIGHLIGHT WAS THE SEMIFINAL DEFEAT BY WEST GERMANY

THE FINAL 11TH JULY, 1982

ITALY 3:1 WEST GERMANY

SANTIAGO BERNABEU STADIUM, MADRID
ATTENDANCE: 90,000
REFEREE: ARNALDO CEZAR COELHO (BRAZIL)

COACH ENZO BEARZOT AND HIS UN-ITALIAN ATTACKING PHILOSOPHY LED THE AZZURRI TO THEIR THIRD WORLD CUP VICTORY

24TH MINUTE
BRIEGEL FOULS CONTI- PENALTY!

CABRINI MISSES

1:0 ROSSI HEADS HOME
57TH MINUTE
calculators
Gillette Gillette

2:0
TARDELLI
69TH MINUTE

3:0 ALTOBELLI
82ND MINUTE
COCA-CO

3:1 BREITNER. A CONSOLATION GOAL
83RD MINUTE

1982 IN OVERVIEW

GROUP 1

DATE	TEAM	R	TEAM
14.06.	ITALY	0:0	POLAND
15.06.	PERU	0:0	CAMEROON
18.06.	ITALY	1:1	PERU
19.06.	POLAND	0:0	CAMEROON
22.06.	POLAND	5:1	PERU
23.06.	ITALY	1:1	CAMEROON

PTS: POLAND 4, ITALY 3, CAMEROON 3, PERU 2

GROUP 2

DATE	TEAM	R	TEAM
16.06.	WEST GERMANY	1:2	ALGERIA
17.06.	CHILE	0:1	AUSTRIA
20.06.	WEST GERMANY	4:1	CHILE
21.06.	ALGERIA	0:2	AUSTRIA
24.06.	ALGERIA	3:2	CHILE
25.06.	WEST GERMANY	1:0	AUSTRIA

PTS: WEST GERMANY 4, AUSTRIA 4, ALGERIA 4, CHILE 0

GROUP 3

DATE	TEAM	R	TEAM
13.06.	ARGENTINA	0:1	BELGIUM
15.06.	HUNGARY	10:1	EL SALVADOR
18.06.	ARGENTINA	4:1	HUNGARY
19.06.	BELGIUM	1:0	EL SALVADOR
22.06.	BELGIUM	1:1	HUNGARY
23.06.	ARGENTINA	2:0	EL SALVADOR

PTS: BELGIUM 5, ARGENTINA 4, HUNGARY 3, EL SALVADOR 0

GROUP 4

DATE	TEAM	R	TEAM
16.06.	ENGLAND	3:1	FRANCE
17.06.	CZECHOSLOVAKIA	1:1	KUWAIT
20.06.	ENGLAND	2:0	CZECHOSLOVAKIA
21.06.	FRANCE	4:1	KUWAIT
24.06.	FRANCE	1:1	CZECHOSLOVAKIA
25.06.	ENGLAND	1:0	KUWAIT

PTS: ENGLAND 6, FRANCE 3, CZECHOSLOVAKIA 2, KUWAIT 1

GROUP 5

DATE	TEAM	R	TEAM
16.06.	SPAIN	1:1	HONDURAS
17.06.	YUGOSLAVIA	0:0	N. IRELAND
20.06.	SPAIN	2:1	YUGOSLAVIA
21.06.	HONDURAS	1:1	N. IRELAND
24.06.	HONDURAS	0:1	YUGOSLAVIA
25.06.	N. IRELAND	1:0	SPAIN

PTS: N. IRELAND 4, SPAIN 3, YUGOSLAVIA 3, HONDURAS 2

GROUP 6

DATE	TEAM	R	TEAM
14.06.	BRAZIL	2:1	USSR
15.06.	SCOTLAND	5:2	NEW ZEALAND
18.06.	BRAZIL	4:1	SCOTLAND
19.06.	USSR	3:0	NEW ZEALAND
22.06.	USSR	2:2	SCOTLAND
23.06.	BRAZIL	4:0	NEW ZEALAND

PTS: BRAZIL 6, USSR 3, SCOTLAND 3, NEW ZEALAND 0

SECOND ROUND

GROUP A

DATE	TEAM	R	TEAM
28.06.	POLAND	3:0	BELGIUM
01.07.	BELGIUM	0:1	USSR
04.07.	POLAND	0:0	USSR

PTS: POLAND 3, USSR 3, BELGIUM 0

GROUP B

DATE	TEAM	R	TEAM
29.06.	WEST GERMANY	0:0	ENGLAND
02.07.	WEST GERMANY	2:1	SPAIN
05.07.	SPAIN	0:0	ENGLAND

PTS: WEST GERMANY 3, ENGLAND 2, SPAIN 1

GROUP C

DATE	TEAM	R	TEAM
29.06.	ITALY	2:1	ARGENTINA
02.07.	ARGENTINA	1:3	BRAZIL
05.07.	ITALY	3:2	BRAZIL

PTS: ITALY 4, BRAZIL 2, ARGENTINA 0

GROUP D

DATE	TEAM	R	TEAM
28.06.	AUSTRIA	0:1	FRANCE
01.07.	AUSTRIA	2:2	N. IRELAND
04.07.	FRANCE	4:1	N. IRELAND

PTS: FRANCE 4, AUSTRIA 1, N. IRELAND 1

SEMIFINAL

DATE	TEAM	R	TEAM
08.07.	POLAND	0:2	ITALY
08.07.	W. GERMANY	3:3 E.T, 5:4 P.	FRANCE

3RD PLACE

DATE	TEAM	R	TEAM
10.07.	POLAND	3:2	FRANCE

FINAL

DATE	TEAM	R	TEAM
11.07.	ITALY	3:1	W. GERMANY

CHAMPION: ITALY

TICKET 1982

QUALIFIED TEAMS
24 (FROM 107 CANDIDATES)

PLAYERS IN FIELD

396

FASTEST GOAL
27 SECONDS: BRYAN ROBSON (ENGLAND–FRANCE)

TOP SCORERS
GOLDEN BOOT, 6 GOALS
PAOLO ROSSI (ITALY)
SILVER BOOT, 5 GOALS
KARL-HEINZ RUMMENIGGE (WEST GERMANY)
BRONZE BOOT, 4 GOALS
ZICO (BRAZIL)

BEST GOALKEEPER
DINO ZOFF (ITALY)

BEST YOUNG PLAYER
MANUEL AMOROS, 21 YEARS (FRANCE)

PERIOD
13TH JUNE, 1982–11TH JULY, 1982

GOALS
146 (Ø: 2.81 PER MATCH)

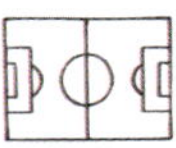

MATCHES
52

FAIR PLAY AWARD
BRAZIL

YELLOW CARDS
98 (Ø: 1.88 PER MATCH)

RED CARDS
5 (Ø: 0.1 PER MATCH)

3 OR MORE GOALS IN A MATCH
3 GOALS: RUMMENIGGE (WEST GERMANY–CHILE), LASZLO KISS (HUNGARY–EL SALVADOR), BONIEK (POLAND–BELGIUM) ROSSI (ITALY–BRAZIL)

ATTENDANCE
2,109,723 (Ø: 40,572 PER MATCH)

OWN GOALS
1

MOST DANGEROUS TEAM
FRANCE: 16 GOALS IN 7 MATCHES

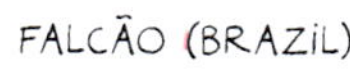

BEST PLAYER TOP 3
GOLDEN BALL
PAOLO ROSSI (ITALY)
SILVER BALL
FALCÃO (BRAZIL)
BRONZE BALL KARL-HEINZ RUMMENIGGE (WEST GERMANY)

PENALTIES
10: 8 SCORED, 2 MISSED

DREAM TEAM 1982

1
10

1986 MEXICO

MARADONA, GOD OF SOCCER TO MANY ARGENTINE PEOPLE, WON THE CUP ALMOST BY HIMSELF, BUT HE INSISTED, "WE ARE A TEAM"

1986 MEXICO

Undoubtedly, 'El diez' (number 10) was an icon of the second World Cup celebrated in Mexico from May 31 to June 29. This tournament has made history due to Diego Armando Maradona´s performance. Or perhaps it was because God put his hand in the field?

It was the first World Cup with 24 teams and a Round of 16. Defending champions Italy (victims of a superb goal by Maradona) were disappointed by being eliminated early by France. In the quarterfinals, "Les Bleus" faced Brazil, and after a thrilling 1–1 draw that lasted through extra time, the penalty shoot-out proved decisive and dramatic: even though Platini missed his penalty, the Europeans advanced to the semifinals 4–3. The second match of the quarter-finals, between England and Argentina, was a classic. In minute six of the second half, Peter Shilton, goalkeeper of England, tried to stop a high ball. Maradona (1.65m) jumped, touched the ball with his hand and chipped it past Shilton. After the match, Diego said, "I touched the ball with my head and a little bit with the hand of God." "It was a totally legal goal, the referee validated it," he told a BBC journalist one year later. Four minutes after that controversial goal, he picked up the ball in his own half, dribbled past the English players at full speed, and scored what would go down in history as The Goal of the Century. Thus, he healed old wounds and gave the Argentine people an everlasting emotion.

In the semifinals, Belgium (after a great tournament) faced a brilliant Maradona and fell 2–0, while West Germany defeated France.

The German team trusted in their capacity to adapt to the high altitude but was beaten in the final by Argentina. Matthäus marked Maradona closely, so he could not fully display his abilities. However, Argentina went 2–0 up until Rummenigge and Völler equalized 2–2 only fifteen minutes from time. Yet there was still time for the magician to wave his wand once more: a counter-attack led by the number 10 and finished by Burruchaga made the dream come true once again for Argentina. They won the match 3–2 and became World Champions for the second time!

'LA MANO DE DIOS' (THE HAND OF GOD)

THE SECOND GOAL THAT MARADONA SCORED WAS CALLED 'THE GOAL OF THE CENTURY'.
THE NO. 10 PICKED UP THE BALL IN HIS OWN HALF, BEAT BEARDSLEY AND REID, DASHED TORWARD ENGLAND'S GOAL. THE CROWD IN THE AZTECA STADIUM HELD ITS COLLECTIVE BREATH AS HE WENT PASS BUTCHER AND FENWICK, ROUNDED PETER SHILTON AND SLOTTED HOME HIS SECOND GOAL.

LEGENDARY COMMENTATOR VICTOR HUGO MORALES DESCRIBED IT IN AN EXCITING WAY THAT WILL ALWAYS BE REMEBERED BY THE FANS IN ARGENTINA. IT ENDED: "THANK YOU GOD FOR SOCCER, FOR MARADONA, FOR THESE TEARS, FOR THIS ARGENTINA 2 , ENGLAND 0."

ENGLISH GOALSCORER GARY LINEKER WON THE GOLDEN BOOT AFTER SCORING SIX TIMES

'THE MEXICAN WAVE' WAS A FEATURE OF THIS TOURNAMENT. NOW, IT HAS BECOME A PHENOMENON IN MANY SPORTS EVENTS

ON HIS 31ST BIRTHDAY, MICHEL PLATINI KISSES THE BALL BEFORE KICKING A PENALTY IN THE MATCH AGAINST BRAZIL. BUT THE SPELL DID NOT COME TO HIS AID. THE BALL FLEW OVER THE BAR. HOWEVER, FRANCE WON THE SHOOT-OUT 4-3 AND COULD CELEBRATE, BUT WENT ON TO LOSE TO WEST GERMANY IN THE SEMIFINAL FOR THE SECOND TIME

AFA
reusch
2
9

1986 WORLD CHAMPIONS: ARGENTINA.
TOP: SERGIO BATISTA, JOSÉ CUCIUFFO, JULIO OLARTICOECHEA, NERY PUMPIDO,
JOSÉ BROWN, OSCAR RUGGERI, DIEGO MARADONA. BOTTOM: JORGE BURRUCH
RICARDO GIUSTI, HÉCTOR ENRIQUE, JORGE VALDANO

MARADONA SCORED AGAINST BELGIUM ANOTHER UNFFORGETTABLE GOAL

CARLOS BILARDO, ARGENTINA'S COACH, WAS CRITICIZED FOR HIS DEFENSIVE TACTICS. BUT AFTER HIS TEAM'S TRIUMPH THERE WERE SIGNS READING: 'PERDÓN BILARDO' (FORGIVE US BILARDO)

THE FINAL 29TH JUNE, 1986

ARGENTINA 3:2 WEST GERMANY

ESTADIO AZTECA, MÉXICO CITY

ATTENDANCE: 114,600

REFEREE: ROMUALDO ARPPI FILHO (BRAZIL)

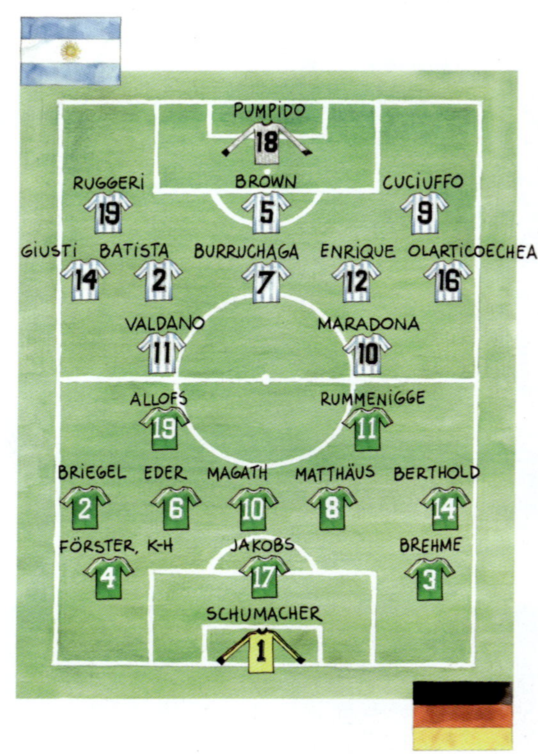

MINE!!! SCHUMACHER FLIES TO CATCH BUTTERFLIES? AS BROWN HEADS HOME (TO AN EMPTY GOAL)

3:2 COUNTERATTACK, A MAGIC PASS FROM MARADONA GIVES BURRUCHAGA THE CHANCE TO SCORE A WINNER

1986 IN OVERVIEW

GROUP A

DATE	TEAM	R	TEAM
31.05.	BULGARIA	1:1	ITALY
02.06.	ARGENTINA	3:1	SOUTH KOREA
05.06.	ITALY	1:1	ARGENTINA
05.06.	SOUTH KOREA	1:1	BULGARIA
10.06.	ARGENTINA	2:0	BULGARIA
10.06.	SOUTH KOREA	2:3	ITALY

PTS: ARGENTINA 5, ITALY 4, BULGARIA 2, SOUTH KOREA 0

GROUP B

DATE	TEAM	R	TEAM
03.06.	BELGIUM	1:2	MEXICO
04.06.	PARAGUAY	1:0	IRAQ
07.06.	MEXICO	1:1	PARAGUAY
08.06.	IRAQ	1:2	BELGIUM
11.06.	PARAGUAY	2:2	BELGIUM
11.06.	IRAQ	0:1	MEXICO

PTS: MEXICO 5, PARAGUAY 4, BELGIUM 3, IRAQ 0

GROUP C

DATE	TEAM	R	TEAM
01.06.	CANADA	0:1	FRANCE
02.06.	USSR	6:0	HUNGARY
05.06.	FRANCE	1:1	USSR
06.06.	HUNGARY	2:0	CANADA
09.06.	USSR	2:0	CANADA
09.06.	HUNGARY	0:3	FRANCE

PTS: USSR 5, FRANCE 5, HUNGARY 2, CANADA 0

GROUP D

DATE	TEAM	R	TEAM
01.06.	SPAIN	0:1	BRAZIL
03.06.	ALGERIA	1:1	N. IRELAND
06.06.	BRAZIL	1:0	ALGERIA
07.06.	N. IRELAND	1:2	SPAIN
12.06.	N. IRELAND	0:3	BRAZIL
12.06.	ALGERIA	0:3	SPAIN

PTS: BRAZIL 6, SPAIN 4, N. IRELAND 1, ALGERIA 1

GROUP E

DATE	TEAM	R	TEAM
04.06.	URUGUAY	1:1	WEST GERMANY
04.06.	SCOTLAND	0:1	DENMARK
08.06.	WEST GERMANY	2:1	SCOTLAND
08.06.	DENMARK	6:1	URUGUAY
13.06.	DENMARK	2:0	WEST GERMANY
13.06.	SCOTLAND	0:0	URUGUAY

PTS: DENMARK 6, W. GERMANY 3, URUGUAY 2, SCOTLAND 1

GROUP F

DATE	TEAM	R	TEAM
02.06.	MOROCCO	0:0	POLAND
03.06.	PORTUGAL	1:0	ENGLAND
06.06.	ENGLAND	0:0	MOROCCO
07.06.	POLAND	1:0	PORTUGAL
11.06.	PORTUGAL	1:3	MOROCCO
11.06.	ENGLAND	3:0	POLAND

PTS: MOROCCO 4, ENGLAND 3, POLAND 2, PORTUGAL 2

ROUND OF 16

DATE	TEAM	R	TEAM
15.06.	MEXICO	2:0	BULGARIA
15.06.	USSR	3:4	BELGIUM
16.06.	BRAZIL	4:0	POLAND
16.06.	ARGENTINA	1:0	URUGUAY
17.06.	ITALY	0:2	FRANCE
17.06.	MOROCCO	0:1	W. GERMANY
18.06.	ENGLAND	3:0	PARAGUAY
18.06.	DENMARK	1:5	SPAIN

QUARTER-FINALS

DATE	TEAM	R	TEAM
21.06.	BRAZIL	1:1 E.T, 3:4 P.	FRANCE
21.06.	W. GERMANY	0:0 E.T, 4:1 P.	MEXICO
22.06.	ARGENTINA	2:1	ENGLAND
22.06.	SPAIN	1:1 E.T, 4:5 P.	BELGIUM

PTS: WEST GERMANY 3, ENGLAND 2, SPAIN 1

SEMIFINALS

DATE	TEAM	R	TEAM
25.06.	FRANCE	0:2	W. GERMANY
25.06.	ARGENTINA	2:0	BELGIUM

3RD PLACE

DATE	TEAM	R	TEAM
28.06.	FRANCE	4:2 E.T	BELGIUM

FINAL

DATE	TEAM	R	TEAM
29.06.	ARGENTINA	3:2	W. GERMANY

TICKET 1986

CHAMPION: ARGENTINA

QUALIFIED TEAMS
24 (FROM 121 CANDIDATES)

PERIOD
31TH MAY, 1986–29TH JUNE, 1986

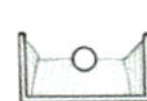

ATTENDANCE
2,394,031 (Ø: 46,039 PER MATCH)

PLAYERS IN FIELD

413

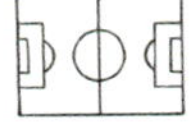

GOALS
132 (Ø: 2.54 PER MATCH)

OWN GOALS
1

FASTEST GOAL
63 SECONDS: BUTRAGUENO
(SPAIN–N. IRELAND)

MATCHES
52

MOST DANGEROUS TEAM
ARGENTINA. 14 GOALS
IN 7 MATCHES

TOP SCORERS
GOLDEN BOOT, 6 GOALS
GARY LINEKER (ENGLAND)
SILVER BOOT, 5 GOALS
EMILIO BUTRAGUEÑO (SPAIN)
CARECA (BRAZIL), DIEGO
MARADONA (ARGENTINA)

FAIR PLAY AWARD
BRAZIL

BEST PLAYER
GOLDEN BALL
DIEGO MARADONA (ARGENTINA)
SILVER BALL
HARALD SCHUMACHER (WEST GERMANY)
BRONZE BALL
PREBEN ELKJÆR LARSEN (DENMARK)

YELLOW CARDS
133 (Ø: 2.56 PER MATCH)

RED CARDS
8 (Ø: 0.15 PER MATCH)

BEST GOALKEEPER
JEAN-MARIE PFAFF (BELGIUM)

3 OR MORE GOALS IN A MATCH
4 GOALS: BUTRAGUEÑO (SPAIN–DENMARK)
3 GOALS: ELKJAER LARSEN (DENMARK–URUGUAY), LINEKER (ENGLAND–POLAND)
BELANOW (SOWJETUNION–BELGIUM)

PENALTIES
14: 12 SCORED, 2 MISSED

BEST YOUNG PLAYER
ENZO SCIFO,
20 YEARS (BELGIUM)

DREAM TEAM 1986

PFAFF
AMOROS
J. CÉSAR
JOSIMAR
MARADONA
CEULEMANS
TIGANA
PLATINI
LINEKER
BUTRAGUEÑO
LARSEN

1990 ITALY

WEST GERMANY TAKES REVENGE AGAINST ARGENTINA FOR THEIR DEFEAT IN 1986. ANDREAS BREHME SCORES THE WINNING GOAL FROM THE PENALTY SPOT

1990 ITALY

During the tournament played from June 8 to July 8, 1990, in Italy, and beginning with the melody of "Un'estate italiana", considered the best World Cup anthem, there are some moments that will remain iconic in the mind of any soccer fan; such as thoughtful Franz Beckenbauer, walking slowly and alone across the pitch of the Stadio Olimpico in Rome, enjoying the victory, while just a few meters away, Diego Armando Maradona cried like a child, devastated over Argentina's defeat.

For the third consecutive time, West Germany had reached the final, having the chance to take revenge for the defeat suffered four years earlier—a situation no previous finalist had ever faced. One of the most iconic moments is the joyful corner-flag dance of veteran Cameroonian Roger Milla, who scored four goals, symbolizing a team that was the surprise of the tournament, reaching the quarter-finals and becoming the first African country to go that far.

The Netherlands had a great team; however, they let their supporters down, since they only reached the round of sixteen, after three draws. Rudi Völler became a victim of Dutch frustration when Frank Rijkaard spat at him. Brazil was knocked out in the first knockout round by Argentina, in a match not for the faint-hearted. Goycochea made several saves! The ball hit the post! Brazil missed a lot of scoring chances. Maradona's magic shows up once more, with an unforgettable move. He assisted Claudio Caniggia who scored the winner in the only chance that came to Argentina's way.

Italy put all its trust in Salvatore Schillaci (Juventus Turin), the little-known attacker who carried the team all the way to the semifinals.

The 1990 tournament is remembered as the penalty shoot-out World Cup. In the quarter-finals, three out of four matches were decided on penalties. The same happened in the semifinals: Argentina against Italy and West Germany against England. Beckenbauer's team and Argentina advanced to the final. And fittingly, the decisive moment of the final also came from the penalty spot: a kick scored by Andreas Brehme in the 85th minute gave Germany both the victory and their third World Cup.

ROGER MILLA´S MEMORABLE DANCE IS STILL INSPIRING THE MOST CREATIVE CELEBRATIONS. IN 1990, THE CAMEROONIAN IDOL CAME BACK FROM RETIREMENT AT THE AGE OF 38 AND CELEBRATED HIS GOALS UNIQUELY

CAMEROON SHOCK 1-0 VICTORY. OMAN BIYIK SCORING THE WINNER AGAINST ARGENTINA, THE DEFENDING CHAMPION

THE COLOMBIAN GOALKEEPER,
RENE HUIGUITA, GOES OUTSIDE THE BOX,
ALMOST UP TO THE MID-FIELD, HE RECEIVES THE BALL AND CANNOT CONTROL IT.
ROGER MILLA TAKES THE BALL FROM HUIGUITA AND SCORES AFTER A RUN

THE ITALIAN STRIKER ROBERTO BAGGIO SCORED AGAINST CZECHOSLOVAKIA THE MOST BEAUTIFUL GOAL OF THE 1990 WORLD CUP

LOTHAR MATTHÄUS, WHO CAPTAINED GERMANY TO VICTORY, IS THE SOCCERER WHO HAS MOST APPEARANCES FOR GERMANY. HE IS ALSO A RECORD CAPS HOLDER FOR HIS NATIONAL TEAM IN THE WORLD CUP HISTORY

IN A REPUGNANT ACT, FRANK RIJKAARD SPIT AT RUDI VÖLLER! BOTH WERE SENT OFF

IN NAPLES, CLAUDIO CANIGGIA EQUALIZES THE SEMIFINAL FOR ARGENTINA. THE SOUTH AMERICANS GO ON TO WIN ON PENALTIES. "THIS IS THE MATCH THAT I ENJOYED THE MOST," MARADONA SAID

TOTO SCHILLACI, TOP SCORER WITH SIX GOALS, COULD NOT UNDERSTAND WHY HE WAS ALWAYS OFFSIDE
?!!
19

1990 WORLD CHAMPIONS: WEST GERMANY.
TOP: HOLGER OSIECK (ASSISTANT), FRANZ BECKENBAUER (COACH), KLAUS AUGENTHALER, STEFAN REUTER, JÜRGEN KLINSMANN, FRANK MILL, GUIDO BUCHWALD, PAUL STEINER, THOMAS BERTHOLD, ANDREAS KÖPKE, JÜRGEN KOHLER, ANDREAS MÖLLER,

HANS PFLÜGLER, BERTI VOGTS (ASSISTANT COACH).
BOTTOM: PIERRE LITTBARSKI, OLAF THON, SEPP MAYER (GOALKEEPER´S COACH), ANDREAS BREHME, LOTHAR MATTHÄUS, KARL-HEINZ RIEDLE, BODO ILLGNER, UWE BEIN, GÜNTHER HERMANN, RUDI VÖLLER, THOMAS HÄSSLER, RAIMOND AUMANN.

WHAT THE ENGLISH REMEMBER THE MOST ABOUT THIS WORLD CUP, ARE GAZZA'S (PAUL GASCOIGNE) DRAMATIC TEARS. HE WAS SOMETIMES CHARISMATIC AND OTHER TIMES CRAZY. HE STARTED TO CRY IN THE SEMIFINAL WHEN REALIZED THAT THE SECOND BOOKING MEANT NOT BEING ABLE TO PLAY AN EVENTUAL FINAL. FINALLY, ENGLAND WAS DEFEATED, BUT HIS CRYING REMAINS IN THE HEART OF THE SUPPORTERS

THE FINAL 8TH JULY, 1990

WEST GERMANY 1:0 ARGENTINA

STADIO OLIMPICO, ROME

ATTENDANCE: 73,603

REFEREE: EDGARDO CODESAL MENDEZ (MEXICO)

FRANZ BECKENBAUER BECOMES THE SECOND MAN WHO WON THE WORLD CUP BOTH AS A PLAYER AND AS A COACH, AFTER MARIO ZAGALLO

65TH MINUTE
MONZON IS SENT OFF AFTER COMMITTING A FOUL ON KLINSMANN WHO DIVES AS A HOLLYWOOD ACTOR

85TH MINUTE
A PENALTY?
VÖLLER DIVES AND THE REFEREE AWARDS HIM A PENALTY

1:0
GOYCOCHEA DIVES TO THE RIGHT SIDE, BUT BREHMES SHOOT-OUT WAS PERFECT

GOOOAL!!! BREHME IS OVERPOWERED BY TEAMMATES

DEZOTTI IS SENT OFF FOR COMMITTING A FOUL ON KOHLER
87TH MINUTE

END OF MATCH
MATTHÄUS CONSOLES MARADONA

...AND THEN CELEBRATES WITH HIS TEAM MATES THE WELL-DESERVED WORLD CUP AFTER BEING DEFEATED IN TWO PREVIOUS FINALS

1990 IN OVERVIEW

GROUP A

DATE	TEAM	R	TEAM
09.06.	ITALY	1:0	AUSTRIA
10.06.	USA	1:5	CZECHOSLOVAKIA
14.06.	ITALY	1:0	USA
15.06.	AUSTRIA	0:1	CZECHOSLOVAKIA
19.06.	ITALY	2:0	CZECHOSLOVAKIA
19.06.	AUSTRIA	2:1	USA

PTS: ITALY 6, CZECHOSLOVAKIA 4, AUSTRIA 2, USA 0

GROUP B

DATE	TEAM	R	TEAM
08.06.	ARGENTINA	0:1	CAMEROON
09.06.	USSR	0:2	ROMANIA
13.06.	ARGENTINA	2:0	USSR
14.06.	CAMEROON	2:1	ROMANIA
18.06.	ARGENTINA	1:1	ROMANIA
18.06.	CAMEROON	0:4	USSR

PTS: CAMEROON 4, ROMANIA 3, ARGENTINA 3, USSR 2

GROUP C

DATE	TEAM	R	TEAM
10.06.	BRAZIL	2:1	SWEDEN
11.06.	COSTA RICA	1:0	SCOTLAND
16.06.	BRAZIL	1:0	COSTA RICA
16.06.	SWEDEN	1:2	SCOTLAND
20.06.	BRAZIL	1:0	SCOTLAND
20.06.	SWEDEN	1:2	COSTA RICA

PTS: BRAZIL 6, COSTA RICA 4, SCOTLAND 2, SWEDEN 0

GROUP D

DATE	TEAM	R	TEAM
09.06.	UA EMIRATES	0:2	COLOMBIA
10.06.	WEST GERMANY	4:1	YUGOSLAVIA
14.06.	YUGOSLAVIA	1:0	COLOMBIA
15.06.	WEST GERMANY	5:1	UAE
19.06.	WEST GERMANY	1:1	COLOMBIA
19.06.	YUGOSLAVIA	4:1	UAE

PTS: W. GERMANY 5, YUGOSLAVIA 4, COLOMBIA 3, UAE 0

GROUP E

DATE	TEAM	R	TEAM
12.06.	BELGIUM	2:0	SOUTH KOREA
13.06.	URUGUAY	0:0	SPAIN
17.06.	SOUTH KOREA	1:3	SPAIN
17.06.	BELGIUM	3:1	URUGUAY
21.06.	BELGIUM	1:2	SPAIN
21.06.	SOUTH KOREA	0:1	URUGUAY

PTS: SPAIN 5, BELGIUM 4, URUGUAY 3, SOUTH KOREA 0

GROUP F

DATE	TEAM	R	TEAM
11.06.	ENGLAND	1:1	REP. IRELAND
12.06.	NETHERLANDS	1:1	EGYPT
16.06.	ENGLAND	0:0	NETHERLANDS
17.06.	REP. IRELAND	0:0	EGYPT
21.06.	ENGLAND	1:0	EGYPT
21.06.	REP. IRELAND	1:1	NETHERLANDS

PTS: ENGLAND 4, REP. IRELAND 3, NETHERLANDS 3, EGYPT 2

ROUND OF 16

DATE	TEAM	R	TEAM
23.06.	CAMEROON	2:1 E.T	COLOMBIA
23.06.	CZECHOSL.	4:1	COSTA RICA
24.06.	BRAZIL	0:1	ARGENTINA
24.06.	W. GERMANY	2:1	NETHERLANDS
25.06.	REP. IRELAND	0:0 E.T, 5:4 P.	ROMANIA
25.06.	ITALY	2:0	URUGUAY
26.06.	SPAIN	1:2 E.T	YUGOSLAVIA
26.06.	ENGLAND	1:0 E.T	BELGIUM

QUARTER-FINALS

DATE	TEAM	R	TEAM
30.06.	YUGOSLAVIA	0:0 E.T 2:3 P.	ARGENTINA
30.06.	ITALY	1:0	REP. IRELAND
01.07.	W. GERMANY	1:0	CZECHOSL.
01.07.	ENGLAND	3:2 E.T	CAMEROON

SEMIFINALS

DATE	TEAM	R	TEAM
03.07.	ITALY	1:1 E.T 3:4 P.	ARGENTINA
04.07.	W. GERMANY	1:1 E.T, 4:3 P.	ENGLAND

3RD PLACE

DATE	TEAM	R	TEAM
07.07.	ITALY	2:1	ENGLAND

FINAL

DATE	TEAM	R	TEAM
08.07.	W. GERMANY	1:0	ARGENTINA

TICKET 1990

QUALIFIED TEAMS
24 (FROM 112 CANDIDATES)

PLAYERS IN FIELD

414

FASTEST GOAL
5 MINUTES: SUSI (YUGOSLAVIA–UNITED ARAB EMIRATES)

TOP SCORERS
GOLDEN BOOT, 6 GOALS
SALVATORE SCHILLACI (ITALY)
SILVER BOOT, 5 GOALS
TOMÁŠ SKUHRAVÝ (CZECHOSLOVAKIA)
BRONZE BOOT, 4 GOALS
ROGER MILLA (CAMEROON)

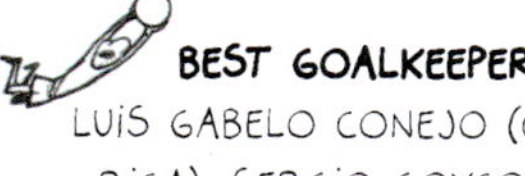

BEST GOALKEEPER
LUIS GABELO CONEJO (COSTA RICA), SERGIO GOYCOCHEA (ARGENTINA)

BEST YOUNG PLAYER
ROBERT PROSINEKI, 21 YEARS (YUGOSLAVIA)

PERIOD
8TH JUNE, 1990–8TH JULY, 1990

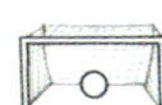

GOALS
115 (Ø: 2.21 PER MATCH)

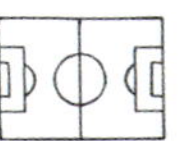

MATCHES
52

FAIR PLAY AWARD
ENGLAND

YELLOW CARDS
162 (Ø: 3.13 PER MATCH)
RED CARDS
16 (Ø: 0.31 PER MATCH)

3 OR MORE GOALS IN A MATCH
3 GOALS: MICHEL (SPAIN–SOUTH KOREA)
SKUHRAVÝ (CZECHOSLOVAKIA–COSTA RICA)

ATTENDANCE
2,516,215 (Ø: 48,389 PER MATCH)

OWN GOALS
0

MOST DANGEROUS TEAM
GERMANY: 15 GOALS IN 7 MATCHES

BEST PLAYER
GOLDEN BALL
SALVATORE SCHILLACI (ITALY)
SILVER BALL
LOTHAR MATTHÄUS (GERMANY)
BRONZE BALL
DIEGO MARADONA (ARGENTINA)

PENALTIES
18: 13 SCORED, 3 MISSED, 2 SAVED

DREAM TEAM 1990

1994 USA

ROBERTO BAGGIO HANGS HIS HEAD AFTER MISSING THE LAST PENALTY OF THE FINAL. TAFFAREL COULD NOT BELIEVE IT

1994 USA

A Soccer World Cup in the country of baseball, American football, and basketball? The choice of the United States as host caused skepticism from the very beginning. Yet it is also the nation of show business: viewership records exceeded all expectations. A total of 143 nations took part in the qualifying phase for the tournament, played from June 17 to July 17, and 3.6 million spectators followed the 52 matches in modern stadiums, stretching from Boston to Orlando.

On the pitch, there were highs and lows, with one of the most boring finals in history, which also marked the return of the World Cup to South America.

England and France did not qualify. Russia entered for the first time after the dissolution of the Soviet Union. The Russians made headlines despite not advancing past the group stage, as Oleg Salenko scored five goals in the 6-1 victory over Cameroon, a feat that still stands as a record today. Romania, led by the great "Maradona of the Carpathians," Gheorghe Hagi, defeated Argentina 3-2 in the round of sixteen (it should be taken into account that the real Maradona could not play since he had failed a drug test). In the next stage, Romania was knocked out after Sweden defeated them by penalties. Bulgaria, helped by the strong Hristo Stoichkov, amazed everybody by reaching the quarter-finals. With a 2-1 final result, Yordan Letschkow former player of the HSV, sent Germany home.

The favorites, the Brazilian team, with its extraordinary attackers, Romário and Bebeto, met all expectations, topped their group, and, on their way past the host United States, the Netherlands, and Sweden, reached the decisive match, where they faced Roberto Baggio, the star of Italy's Azzurra. The Seleção dominated the match in the first final decided by a penalty shoot-out. This victory gave Brazil its fourth World Cup. Unfortunately, it was Baggio who blazed his penalty over the bar. This caused psychological trauma that kept him in therapy for ages.

ROMÁRIO WANTS TO STAY NEXT TO THE CUP. BRAZIL WINS THE CUP AFTER 24 YEARS

A FAMOUS CELEBRATION IS BORN: BEBETO BRINGS HIS ARMS TOGETHER AND PRETENDS TO CRADLE A BABY AS HOMAGE TO HIS NEWBORN SON. WITH HIM ARE MAZINHO AND ROMÁRIO

DIANA ROSS

DURING THE OPENING CEREMONY, THE SINGER DIANA ROSS SHOWS WHAT SOCCER MEANT FOR THE UNITED STATES OF AMERICA BY KICKING THE WORST PENALTY EVER

THE ROUND OF SIXTEEN MATCH, BULGARIA AGAINST MEXICO WAS SUCH A BORING GAME THAT EVEN THE GOAL POST GOT BORED AND THEY HAD TO CHANGE IT

AL-OWAIRAN, FROM SAUDI ARABIA, SCORED A SPECTACULAR GOAL AGAINST BELGIUM

SAEED AL OWAIRAN

SAEED AL OWAIRAN

SAEED AL OWAIRAN

SAEED AL OWAIRAN

SAEED AL OWAIRAN

HRISTO STOICHKOV, THE STAR OF THE BULGARIAN TEAM THAT QUALIFIED FOR THE SEMIFINAL FOR THE FIRST TIME, AND THE RUSSIAN OLEG SALENKO SHARE THE GOLDEN BOOT AFTER SCORING SIX GOALS. SALENKO SCORED FIVE GOALS AGAINST CAMEROON – A NEW RECORD. IN THE SAME MATCH, ROGER MILLA, AGED 42, SCORED FOR CAMEROON AND BECAME THE OLDEST PLAYER SCORING IN A WORLD CUP

MARADONA´S GREAT CAREER IN THE WORLD CUPS FINISHES AFTER FAILING A DRUG TEST. A FEW HOURS LATER, IN AN INTERVIEW MARADONA SAID, "THEY CUT MY LEGS OFF"

THE COLOMBIAN ANDRES ESCOBAR SCORED AN OWN GOAL IN ONE OF THE GROUP STAGE MATCHES. COLOMBIA WAS DEFEATED 2-1 AGAINST USA. THIS OWN GOAL HAD FATAL CONSEQUENCES. COLOMBIA WAS ELIMINATED AND TEN DAYS LATER ESCOBAR WAS KILLED

YORDAN LETSCHKOW HEADS HOME; THE WINNER FOR BULGARIA IN QUARTER-FINALS AGAINST GERMANY

LEONARDO OF BRAZIL, GENERALLY RECOGNISED AS ONE OF SOCCER'S GENTLEMEN, WAS SENT OFF FOR ELBOWING TAB RAMOS OF THE USA. HE WAS SUSPENDED FOR THE REST OF THE TOURNAMENT

reusch
UMBRO
2
13
5
17
11
8
C
DE FUTEBOL

1994 WORLD CHAMPIONS: BRAZIL.
TOP: TAFFAREL, JORGINHO, ALDAIR, MAURO SILVA, MARCIO SANTOS
BRANCO. BOTTOM: MAZINHO, ROMÁRIO, DUNGA, BEBETO, ZINHO

ROBERTO BAGGIO NICKNAMED 'THE DIVINE PONYTAIL' DUE TO HIS HAIRCUT AND FOR TURNING TO BUDDHISM

CARLOS PARREIRA INSTILED A NEW ATTITUDE INTO THE BRAZILIAN TEAM. INSTEAD OF PLAYING A BEAUTIFUL SOCCER, HIS TEAM HAD TO PLAY BOTH IN A DEFENSIVE AND FUNCTIONAL WAY

THE FINAL 17TH JULY, 1994

BRAZIL 0:0 ITALY (EXTRA-TIME)

PENALTY SHOOT-OUT 3:2

ROSE BOWL, PASADENA

ATTENDANCE: 94, 194

REFEREE: SÁNDOR PUHL (HUNGARY)

AFTER 120 BORING MINUTES, THE FIRST PENALTY SHOOT-OUT IN A WORLD CUP FINAL
BARESI 0-0 FAILS
MARCIO SANTOS (PAGLIUCA SAVES IT)
ALBERTINI 0-1
ROMÁRIO 1-1
EVANI 1-2
BRANCO 2-2
MASSARO 2-2 (TAFFAREL SAVES IT)
TAFFAREL
DUNGA 3-2
PAGLIUCA
BAGGIO PUTS THE BALL IN ITS PLACE...
...SHOOTS AND HE SKIES THE BALL
BRAZIL CHAMPION!!!

1994 IN OVERVIEW

GROUP A

DATE	TEAM	R	TEAM
18.06.	USA	1:1	SWITZERLAND
18.06.	COLOMBIA	1:3	ROMANIA
22.06.	ROMANIA	1:4	SWITZERLAND
22.06.	USA	2:1	COLOMBIA
26.06.	USA	0:1	ROMANIA
26.06.	SWITZERLAND	0:2	COLOMBIA

PTS: ROMANIA 6, SWITZERLAND 4, USA 4, COLOMBIA 3

GROUP B

DATE	TEAM	R	TEAM
19.06.	CAMEROON	2:2	SWEDEN
20.06.	BRAZIL	2:0	RUSSIA
24.06.	BRAZIL	3:0	CAMEROON
24.06.	SWEDEN	3:1	RUSSIA
28.06.	RUSSIA	6:1	CAMEROON
28.06.	BRAZIL	1:1	SWEDEN

PTS: BRAZIL 7, SWEDEN 5, RUSSIA 3, CAMEROON 1

GROUP C

DATE	TEAM	R	TEAM
17.06.	GERMANY	1:0	BOLIVIA
17.06.	SPAIN	2:2	SOUTH KOREA
21.06.	GERMANY	1:1	SPAIN
23.06.	SOUTH KOREA	0:0	BOLIVIA
27.06.	BOLIVIA	1:3	SPAIN
27.06.	GERMANY	3:2	SOUTH KOREA

PTS: GERMANY 7, SPAIN 5, SOUTH KOREA 2, BOLIVIA 1

GROUP D

DATE	TEAM	R	TEAM
21.06.	ARGENTINA	4:0	GREECE
21.06.	NIGERIA	3:0	BULGARIA
25.06.	ARGENTINA	2:1	NIGERIA
26.06.	BULGARIA	4:0	GREECE
30.06.	GREECE	0:2	NIGERIA
30.06.	ARGENTINA	0:2	BULGARIA

PTS: NIGERIA 6, BULGARIA 6, ARGENTINA 6, GREECE 0

GROUP E

DATE	TEAM	R	TEAM
18.06.	ITALY	0:1	IRELAND
19.06.	NORWAY	1:0	MEXICO
23.06.	ITALY	1:0	NORWAY
24.06.	MEXICO	2:1	IRELAND
28.06.	IRELAND	0:0	NORWAY
28.06.	ITALY	1:1	MEXICO

PTS: MEXICO 4, IRELAND 4, ITALY 4, NORWAY 4

GROUP F

DATE	TEAM	R	TEAM
19.06.	BELGIUM	1:0	MOROCCO
20.06.	NETHERLANDS	2:1	SAUDI ARABIA
25.06.	BELGIUM	1:0	NETHERLANDS
25.06.	SAUDI ARABIA	2:1	MOROCCO
29.06.	MOROCCO	1:2	NETHERLANDS
29.06.	BELGIUM	0:1	SAUDI ARABIA

PTS: NETHERLANDS 6, SAUDI ARABIA 6, BELGIUM 6, MOROCCO 0

ROUND OF 16

DATE	TEAM	R	TEAM
02.07.	GERMANY	3:2	BELGIUM
02.07.	SPAIN	3:0	SWITZERLAND
03.07.	SAUDI ARABIA	1:3	SWEDEN
03.07.	ROMANIA	3:2	ARGENTINA
04.07.	NETHERLANDS	2:0	IRELAND
04.07.	BRAZIL	1:0	USA
05.07.	NIGERIA	1:2 E.T	ITALY
04.07.	MEXICO	1:1 E.T, 1:3 P.	BULGARIA

QUARTER-FINALS

DATE	TEAM	R	TEAM
09.07.	ITALY	2:1	SPAIN
09.07.	NETHERLANDS	2:3	BRAZIL
10.07.	BULGARIA	2:1	GERMANY
10.07.	ROMANIA	2:2 E.T, 4:5 P.	SWEDEN

SEMIFINALS

DATE	TEAM	R	TEAM
13.07.	BULGARIA	1:2	ITALY
13.07.	SWEDEN	0:1	BRAZIL

3RD PLACE

DATE	TEAM	R	TEAM
16.07.	SWEDEN	4:0	BULGARIA

FINAL

DATE	TEAM	R	TEAM
17.07.	BRAZIL	0:0 E.T, 3:2 P.	ITALY

TICKET 1994

QUALIFIED TEAMS

24 (FROM 143 CANDIDATES)

PLAYERS IN FIELD

427

FASTEST GOAL

2 MINUTES: GABRIEL BATISTUTA (ARGENTINA–GREECE)

TOP SCORERS

GOLDEN BOOT, 6 GOALS

OLEG SALENKO (RUSSIA), HRISTO STOICHKOV (BULGARIA)

BRONZE BOOT, 5 GOALS

ANDERSSON (SWEDEN), ROMARIO (BRAZIL)

BEST GOALKEEPER

MICHEL PREUD'HOMME (BELGIUM)

BEST YOUNG PLAYER

MARC OVERMARS, 21 YEARS (NETHERLANDS)

PERIOD

17TH JUNE, 1994–17TH JULY, 1994

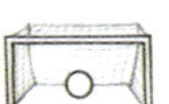

GOALS

141 (Ø: 2.71 PER MATCH)

MATCHES

52

FAIR PLAY AWARD

1. BRAZIL

YELLOW CARDS

228 (Ø: 4.38 PER MATCH)

YELLOW-RED CARDS

7 (Ø: 0.13 PER MATCH)

RED CARDS

8 (Ø: 0.15 PER MATCH)

3 OR MORE GOALS IN A MATCH

5 GOALS: SALENKO (RUSSIA–CAMEROON)

3 GOALS: BATISTUTA (ARGENTINA–GREECE)

ATTENDANCE

3,587,538 (Ø: 68,991 PER MATCH)

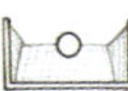

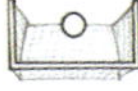

OWN GOALS

1

TORGEFÄHRLICHSTE MANNSCHAFT

SWEDEN: 15 GOALS IN 7 MATCHES

BEST PLAYER

GOLDEN BALL

ROMÁRIO (BRAZIL)

SILVER BALL

ROBERTO BAGGIO (ITALY)

BRONZE BALL

HRISTO STOICHKOV (BULGARIA)

PENALTIES

15: ALL SCORED

DREAM TEAM 1994

1998 FRANCE

RONALDO, WHO WAS ABSOLUTELY CONFUSED IN THE FINAL, COLLIDES WITH THE FRENCH GOALKEEPER FABIEN BARTHEZ

1998 FRANCE

After 60 years, 'La Grande Nation' could host a World Cup again. The tournament took place in France from June 10 to July 12. This World Cup saw the emergence of two new players who would be the new soccer stars. One was from Brazil, and the other from England. 32 teams participated in the final stage, a new dimension never seen before.

The host country started really well. The extraordinary national team became the most successful one in the history of France: Henry, Trezeguet, Djorkaeff, Barthez, Desailly, Thuram and the fascinating Zinédine Zidane. 'Zizou', in his first World Cup, took the lead of his team and led 'Les Bleus' to the final.

In the round of sixteen, something unforgettable happened. In the match against Argentina, Michael Owen, aged 18, slalomed as Maradona used to do, and scored for England. This marked his rise as a fantastic soccer player! On the other hand, David Beckham, who was playing his first World Cup, was the antihero of this match. He was sent off after committing an intentional foul, and both his fans and the press considered this as the reason for the subsequent elimination of England. The Mirror headline said, "Ten heroic lions, one stupid boy." His career bottomed out, but the elite, model, photographic icon and jet set lover player recovered quickly and he later became an idol.

The German national team was not that amazing. In the quarter-finals, Germany faced Croatia, which had recently formed its own national team. Davor Suker's team took advantage of the numerical inferiority of Germany, and sent them packing after a 3-0 final score.

The great striker Ronaldo, aged 21, had scored four goals, and soccer lovers were delighted seeing him in action during the World Cup. In the final match against France, Ronaldo seemed worn out, and was not fit to play. He still played the match. It is said that his sponsor put him under great pressure. France humiliated Brazil. Zidane headed home twice, and Petit scored the third goal: the final result was 3-0.

ZINEDINE ZIDANE, WORTHY SUCCESSOR OF THE NUMBER 10 SOCCER SHIRT THAT WAS WORN BY LEGENDS SUCH AS PELÉ AND MARADONA

CROATIA QUALIFIES FOR THE FIRST TIME FOR A WORLD CUP AND ITS STRIKER DAVOR ŠUKER WINS THE GOLDEN BOOT, AFTER SCORING SIX GOALS

THE ARGENTINE GABRIEL BATISTUTA SET A NEW RECORD AGAINST JAMAICA; HE SCORES A HAT-TRICK IN TWO DIFFERENT WORLD CUPS

THE FRENCH PLAYER LAURENT BLANC SCORED THE FIRST GOLDEN GOAL IN WORLD CUP HISTORY AGAINST PARAGUAY, WINNING THE MATCH 1-0

THE FRENCH KISS OF LUCK: BEFORE EACH MATCH, LAURENT BLANC KISSED GOALKEEPER FABIEN BARTHEZ'S HEAD. ALTHOUGH THE DEFENDER MISSED THE FINAL DUE TO SUSPENSION, HE STILL CARRIED OUT HIS RITUAL, AND FRANCE ENDED UP LIFTING THE CUP

OWEN'S GOAL

OWEN, AGED 18, SCORES. MICHAEL OWEN'S SUBLIME FINISH AGAINST ARGENTINA WILL ALWAYS BE REMEMBERED IN THE HISTORY OF THE CLASSIC OF CLASSICS. THE MATCH ENDED IN A 2-2 DRAW AND ARGENTINA DEFEATED ENGLAND ON PENALTIES

DAVID BECKHAM

A NEW CHAPTER IN THE ETERNAL RIVALRY BETWEEN ARGENTINA AND ENGLAND. DIEGO SIMEONE FOULED DAVID BECKHAM, WHO REACTED BY KICKING OUT AT SIMEONE. SIMEONE WAS PRONE ON THE GROUND AS IF HE HAD BEEN SHOT. BECKHAM IS SENT OFF

AFTER BEATING ENGLAND, ARGENTINA WAS KNOCKED OUT DUE TO THE AWESOME LAST-MINUTE GOAL SCORED BY THE DUTCH PLAYER DENNIS BERGKAMP

COUPE DU MONDE
"FRANCE 98"
BRASIL - FRANCE
FFF
FINALE
STADE DE FRANCE
12 JUILLET 1998

1998 WORLD CHAMPIONS: FRANCE.
TOP: ZINEDINE ZIDANE, MARCEL DESAILLY, FRANK LEBOEUF, LILIAN THURAM
STEPHANE GUIVARC'H, EMMANUEL PETIT. BOTTOM: CHRISTIAN KAREMBEU,
YOURI DJORKAEFF, DIDIER DESCHAMPS, FABIEN BARTHEZ, BIXENTE LIZARA

FRENCH DEFENDER, LILI/
THURAM, BY SCORING TW
GOALS WHEN LOSING T
MATCH 1-0, SAVES FRANCE
THE SEMIFINAL AGAIN
CROATIA. HE ONLY SCORI
TWICE IN 142 INTERNATION
MATCHI

THE CROWD IN PARIS CELEBRATING THE VICTORY

THE FINAL 12TH JULY, 1998

BRAZIL 0:3 FRANCE

STADE DE FRANCE, SAINT-DENIS
ATTENDANCE: 75,000
REFEREE: SAID BELQOLA (MOROCCO)

THE FRENCH COACH AIME JACQUET

IS RONALDO IN THE TEAM SHEET OR NOT?

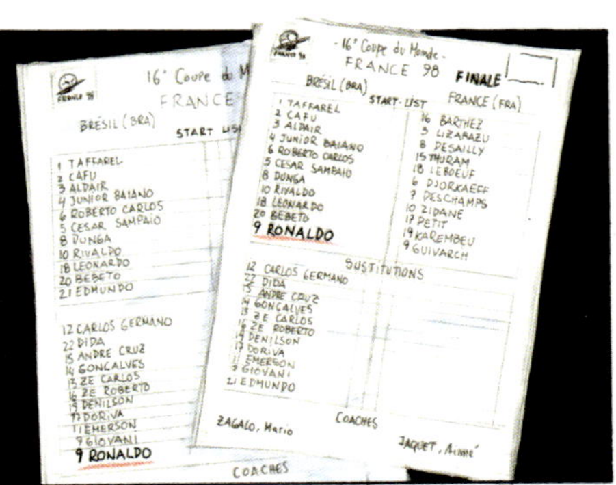

1998 IN OVERVIEW

GROUP A

DATE	TEAM	R	TEAM
10.06.	BRAZIL	2:1	SCOTLAND
10.06.	MOROCCO	2:2	NORWAY
16.06.	SCOTLAND	1:1	NORWAY
16.06.	BRAZIL	3:0	MOROCCO
23.06.	SCOTLAND	0:3	MOROCCO
23.06.	BRAZIL	1:2	NORWAY

PTS: BRAZIL 6, NORWAY 5, MOROCCO 4, SCOTLAND 1

GROUP B

DATE	TEAM	R	TEAM
11.06.	CAMEROON	1:1	AUSTRIA
11.06.	ITALY	2:2	CHILE
17.06.	CHILE	1:1	AUSTRIA
17.06.	ITALY	3:0	CAMEROON
23.06.	ITALY	2:1	AUSTRIA
23.06.	CHILE	1:1	CAMEROON

PTS: ITALY 7, CHILE 3, AUSTRIA 2, CAMEROON 2

GROUP C

DATE	TEAM	R	TEAM
12.06.	SAUDI ARABIA	0:1	DENMARK
12.06.	FRANCE	3:0	SOUTH AFRICA
18.06.	FRANCE	4:0	SAUDI ARABIA
18.06.	SOUTH AFRICA	1:1	DENMARK
24.06.	FRANCE	2:1	DENMARK
24.06.	SOUTH AFRICA	2:2	SAUDI ARABIA

PTS: FRANCE 9, DENMARK 4, SOUTH AFRICA 2, SAUDI ARABIA 1

GROUP D

DATE	TEAM	R	TEAM
12.06.	PARAGUAY	0:0	BULGARIA
13.06.	SPAIN	2:3	NIGERIA
19.06.	NIGERIA	1:0	BULGARIA
19.06.	SPAIN	0:0	PARAGUAY
24.06.	SPAIN	6:1	BULGARIA
24.06.	NIGERIA	1:3	PARAGUAY

PTS: NIGERIA 6, PARAGUAY 5, SPAIN 4, BULGARIA 1

GROUP E

DATE	TEAM	R	TEAM
13.06.	NETHERLANDS	0:0	BELGIUM
13.06.	SOUTH KOREA	1:3	MEXICO
20.06.	NETHERLANDS	5:0	SOUTH KOREA
20.06.	BELGIUM	2:2	MEXICO
25.06.	BELGIUM	1:1	SOUTH KOREA
25.06.	NETHERLANDS	2:2	MEXICO

PTS: NETHERLANDS 5, MEXICO 5, BELGIUM 3, SOUTH KOREA 1

GROUP F

DATE	TEAM	R	TEAM
14.06.	YUGOSLAVIA	1:0	IRAN
15.06.	GERMANY	2:0	USA
21.06.	GERMANY	2:2	YUGOSLAVIA
21.06.	USA	1:2	IRAN
25.06.	GERMANY	2:0	IRAN
25.06.	USA	0:1	YUGOSLAVIA

PTS: GERMANY 7, YUGOSLAVIA 7, IRAN 3, USA 0

GROUP G

DATE	TEAM	R	TEAM
15.06.	ROMANIA	1:0	COLOMBIA
15.06.	ENGLAND	2:0	TUNISIA
22.06.	COLOMBIA	1:0	TUNISIA
22.06.	ROMANIA	2:1	ENGLAND
26.06.	ROMANIA	1:1	TUNISIA
26.06.	COLOMBIA	0:2	ENGLAND

PTS: ROMANIA 7, ENGLAND 6, COLOMBIA 3, TUNISIA 1

GROUP H

DATE	TEAM	R	TEAM
14.06.	JAMAICA	1:3	CROATIA
14.06.	ARGENTINA	1:0	JAPAN
20.06.	JAPAN	0:1	CROATIA
21.06.	ARGENTINA	5:0	JAMAICA
26.06.	JAPAN	1:2	JAMAICA
26.06.	ARGENTINA	1:0	CROATIA

PTS: ARGENTINA 9, CROATIA 6, JAMAICA 3, JAPAN 0

ROUND OF 16

DATE	TEAM	R	TEAM
27.06.	BRAZIL	4:1	CHILE
27.06.	ITALY	1:0	NORWAY
28.06.	NIGERIA	1:4	DENMARK
28.06.	FRANCE	1:0 E.T	PARAGUAY
29.06.	GERMANY	2:1	MEXICO
29.06.	NETHERLANDS	2:1	YUGOSLAVIA
30.06.	ARGENTINA	2:2 E.T, 4:3 P.	ENGLAND
30.06.	ROMANIA	0:1	CROATIA

QUARTER-FINALS

DATE	TEAM	R	TEAM
03.07.	ITALY	0:0 E.T, 3:4 P.	FRANCE
03.07.	BRAZIL	3:2	DENMARK
04.07.	GERMANY	0:3	CROATIA
04.07.	NETHERLANDS	2:1	ARGENTINA

SEMIFINALS

DATE	TEAM	R	TEAM
07.07.	BRAZIL	1:1 E.T, 4:2 P.	NETHERLANDS
08.07.	FRANCE	2:1	CROATIA

3RD PLACE

DATE	TEAM	R	TEAM
11.07.	NETHERLANDS	1:2	CROATIA

FINAL

DATE	TEAM	R	TEAM
12.07.	BRAZIL	0:3	FRANCE

CHAMPION: FRANCE

QUALIFIED TEAMS
32 (FROM 166 CANDIDATES)

PLAYERS IN FIELD
573

FASTEST GOAL
52 SECONDS: AYALA (PARAGUAY–NIGERIA)

TOP SCORERS
GOLDEN BOOT, 6 GOALS
DAVOR ŠUKER (CROATIA)
SILVER BOOT, 5 GOALS
BATISTUTA (ARGENTINA), VIERI (ITALY)

BEST GOALKEEPER
FABIEN BARTHEZ (FRANCE), JOSÉ LUIS CHILAVERT (PARAGUAY)

BEST YOUNG PLAYER
MICHAEL OWEN, 18 YEARS (ENGLAND)

PERIOD
10TH JUNE, 1998–12TH JULY, 1998

GOALS
171 (Ø: 2.67 PER MATCH)

OWN GOALS
7

FAIR PLAY AWARD
1. FRANCE AND ENGLAND
3. NORWAY

YELLOW CARDS
250 (Ø: 3.91 PER MATCH)

YELLOW-RED CARDS
4 (Ø: 0.06 PER MATCH)

RED CARDS
22 (Ø: 0.28 PER MATCH)

3 OR MORE GOALS IN A MATCH
3 GOALS: BATISTUTA (ARGENTINA–JAMAICA)

ATTENDANCE
2,785,100 (Ø: 43,517 PER MATCH)

MATCHES
64

MOST DANGEROUS TEAM
FRANCE: 15 GOALS IN 7 MATCHES

BEST PLAYER
GOLDEN BALL
RONALDO (BRAZIL)
SILVER BALL
DAVOR ŠUKER, (CROATIA)
BRONZE BALL
LILIAN THURAM (FRANCE)

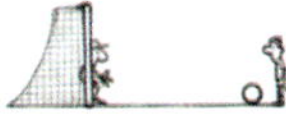

PENALTIES
18: 17 SCORED, 1 MISSED

DREAM TEAM 1998

2002 SOUTH KOREA/JAPAN

RONALDO'S REAPPEARANCE.
THE 2002 BIG STAR HELPED BRAZIL LIFT
ITS FIFTH WORLD CUP

2002 SOUTH KOREA/JAPAN

The 2002 World Cup took place from 31 May to 30 June in South Korea and Japan. It was the first World Cup in history organized by two Asian countries and the first one to be held on a continent other than Europe or the Americas. After two severe knee surgeries, Ronaldo contemplated hanging up his boots. But just as the Phoenix, he arose and became crucial for lifting Brazil's fifth World Cup. 'O Fenômeno' was back.

One of the highlights of this World Cup was the opening match where France, the Champion of the World and Europe, was defeated 1-0 by Senegal, who participated in a World Cup for the first time. The French could not change the course of their campaign, and were knocked out in the opening stage without scoring a goal.

There were certain prejudices about South Korea, since it was not a country with a soccer tradition. The co-host country defeated Portugal, one of the favorite teams, then eliminated Italy with some help from the referee, in the round of sixteen. They defeated Spain in the quarter-finals on penalties. But Michael Ballack put an end to the South Korean team's winning streak, by scoring the winner in the semifinals.

To the joy of England, Argentina was sent home in the first stage. It was David Beckham who contributed to the elimination. Beckham, who had been publicly criticized four years earlier for his performance against an eternal rival, scored the winner from the penalty spot, and could dissipate the anger. England went on to lose to the eventual winners in the quarter-finals. Turkey took the third place, in its second appearance in a World Cup. Germany defeated Paraguay, the United States, and South Korea with identical 1-0 victories to advance into the final. They were up against Brazil, the runners-up in France. Ronaldo had scored amazing goals during the tournament, and the young Ronaldinho delighted everybody with his magic. German goalkeeper Oliver Kahn, who had contributed enormously with his saves up to that point, had a miserable performance in the final in Yokohama; his mistake allowed the opening goal, and he could do nothing to prevent the 2-0 score, both scored by Ronaldo. While "the titan" cried leaning against the post, Brazil lifted their fifth World Cup.

THE GERMAN OLIVER KAHN, AS FAMOUS AS HE WAS FEARED, WAS THE ONLY GOALKEEPER TO BE NAMED THE BEST PLAYER OF THE TOURNAMENT. HOWEVER, IT WAS HIS MISTAKE THAT GAVE THE TITLE TO BRAZIL

DAVID BECKHAM, BY SCORING THE WINNER AGAINST ARGENTINA, TOOK REVENGE FOR THE 1998 SENDING OFF, AND CONTRIBUTED TO THE ELIMINATION OF ARGENTINA IN THE GROUP STAGE

WHAT A GREAT PERFORMANCE! RONALDINHO CELEBRATES BY SEEING HOW DAVID SEEMAN TRIES TO SAVE HIS STUNNING FREE KICK. BRAZIL EVENTUALLY DEFEATED ENGLAND 2-1 IN THE QUARTER-FINALS

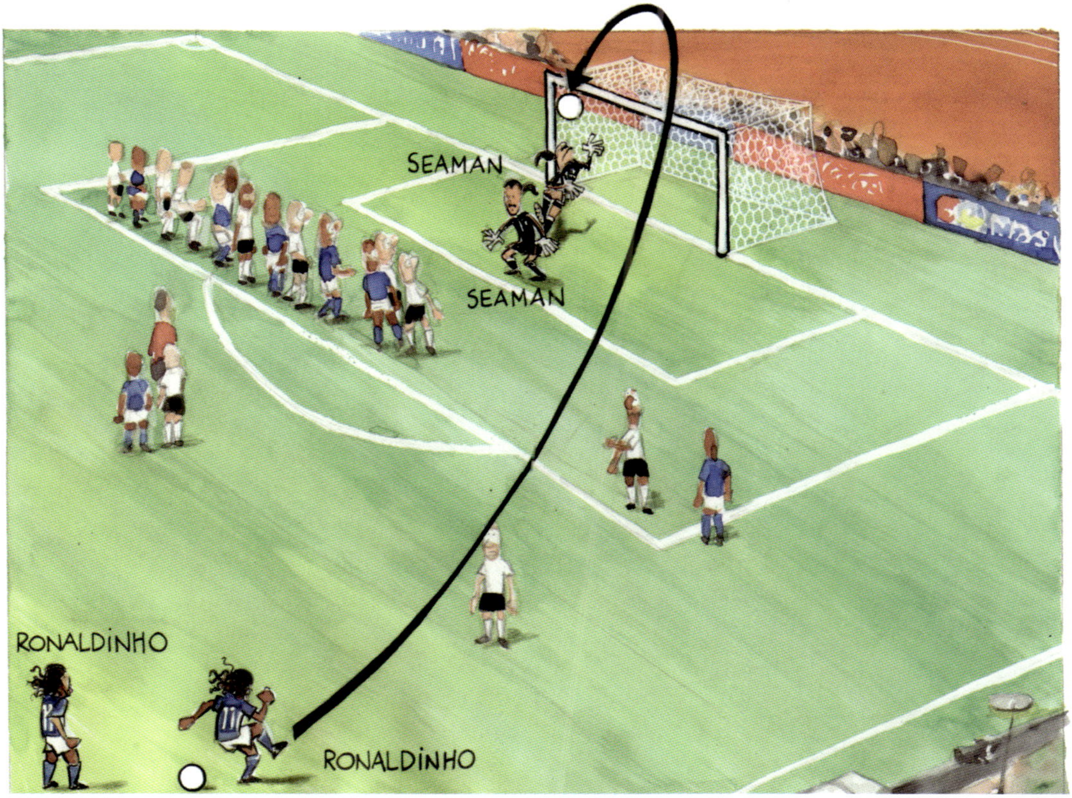

THE BRAZILIAN PLAYER RIVALDO ACTS LIKE A REAL PROFESSIONAL ACTOR AND THE REFEREE SENDS OFF THE TURKISH PLAYER ÜNSAL

BY COMPETING AGAIN THE TWO TEAMS IN THE SEMIFINALS, A SIMPLE TOE POKE FROM RONALDO WAS ENOUGH TO WIN THE MATCH. THE BRAZILIAN PLAYER WON THE GOLDEN BOOT AFTER SCORING EIGHT GOALS...

IT'S A GOLDEN GOAL! AHN JUNG-HWAN HEADS HOME AND ELIMINATES ITALY FROM THE WORLD CUP. THIS MADE THE ITALIANS RECALL THEIR DEFEAT AGAINST NORTH KOREA IN 1966

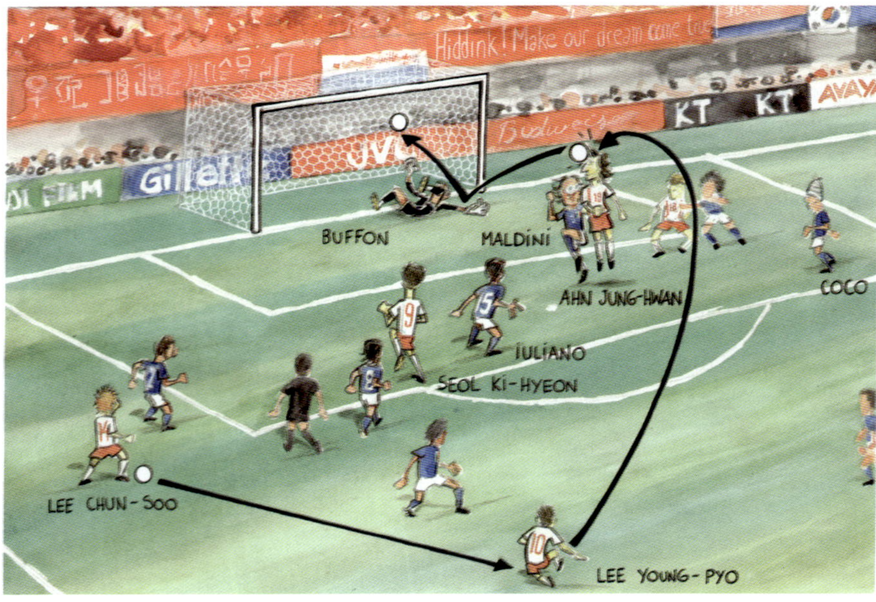

AFTER A FOUL ON SOUTH KOREA'S LEE CHUN-SOO, BALLACK RECEIVES A YELLOW CARD. SO, HE MISSES THE FINAL. BUT FOUR MINUTES LATER, HE HEROICALLY SCORED THE WINNER AND GERMANY ADVANCED TO THE FINAL THAT BALLACK COULD NOT PLAY

2002 WORLD CHAMPIONS: BRAZIL.
TOP: LÚCIO, EDMILSON, ROQUE JÚNIOR, GILBERTO SILVA, MARCOS.
BOTTOM: RONALDINHO, RONALDO, ROBERTO CARLOS, KLEBERSON, RIVALDO, CAFU

FASTEST GOAL

ALTHOUGH SOUTH KOREA KICKED OFF, HAKAN SÜKÜR, SCORED THE FASTEST GOAL IN WORLD CUP HISTORY IN THE THIRD-PLACE PLAY AGAINST SOUTH KOREA

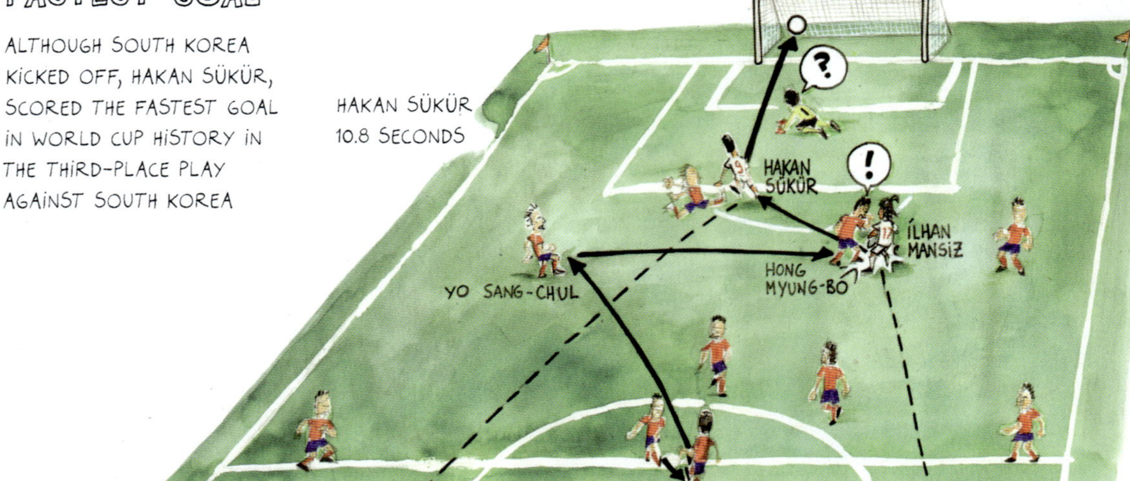

LUIZ FELIPE SCOLARI ´FELIPÃO´
COACH OF BRAZIL

THE FINAL 30TH JUNE, 2002

ALEMANIA 0:2 BRAZIL

INTERNATIONAL STADIUM, YOKOHAMA
ATTENDANCE: 69,029
REFEREE: PIERLUIGI COLLINA (ITALY)

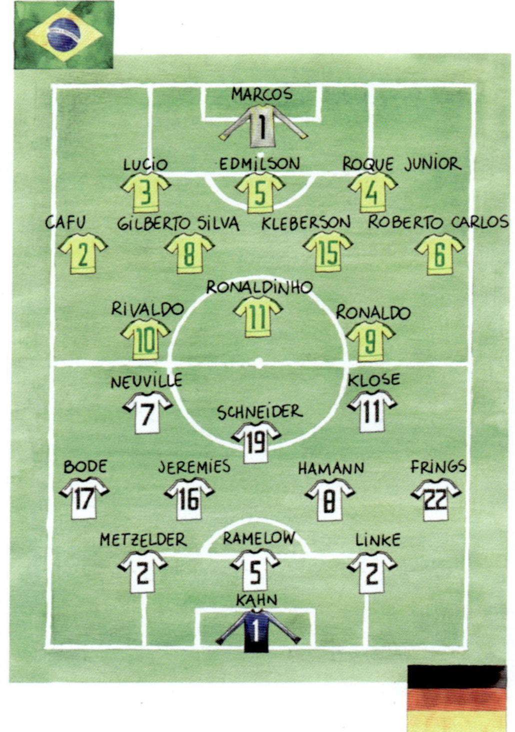

OLIVER KHAN FAILS TO HOLD A HARMLESS SHOT FROM RIVALDO...

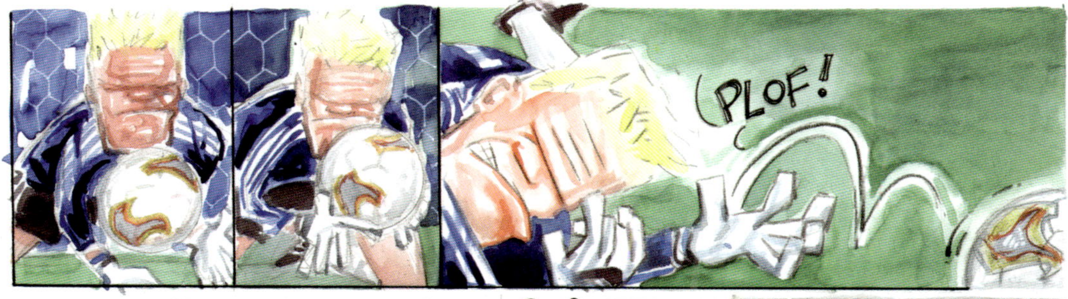

2002 IN OVERVIEW

GROUP A

DATE	TEAM	R	TEAM
31.05.	FRANCE	0:1	SENEGAL
01.06.	URUGUAY	1:2	DENMARK
06.06.	FRANCE	0:0	URUGUAY
06.06.	DENMARK	1:1	SENEGAL
11.06.	DENMARK	2:0	FRANCE
11.06.	SENEGAL	3:3	URUGUAY

PTS: DENMARK 7, SENEGAL 5, URUGUAY 2, FRANCE 1

GROUP B

DATE	TEAM	R	TEAM
02.06.	PARAGUAY	2:2	SOUTH AFRICA
02.06.	SPAIN	3:1	SLOVENIA
07.06.	SPAIN	3:1	PARAGUAY
08.06.	SOUTH AFRICA	1:0	SLOVENIA
12.06.	SOUTH AFRICA	2:3	SPAIN
12.06.	SLOVENIA	1:3	PARAGUAY

PTS: SPAIN 9, PARAGUAY 4, SOUTH AFRICA 4, SLOVENIA 0

GROUP C

DATE	TEAM	R	TEAM
03.06.	BRAZIL	2:1	TURKEY
04.06.	CHINA	0:2	COSTA RICA
08.06.	BRAZIL	4:0	CHINA
09.06.	COSTA RICA	1:1	TURKEY
13.06.	COSTA RICA	2:5	BRAZIL
13.06.	TURKEY	3:0	CHINA

PTS: BRAZIL 9, TURKEY 4, COSTA RICA 4, CHINA 0

GROUP D

DATE	TEAM	R	TEAM
04.06.	SOUTH KOREA	2:0	POLAND
05.06.	USA	3:2	PORTUGAL
10.06.	SOUTH KOREA	1:1	USA
10.06.	PORTUGAL	4:0	POLAND
14.06.	PORTUGAL	0:1	SOUTH KOREA
14.06.	POLAND	3:1	USA

PTS: SOUTH KOREA 7, USA 4, PORTUGAL 3, POLAND 3

GROUP E

DATE	TEAM	R	TEAM
01.06.	IRELAND	1:1	CAMEROON
01.06.	GERMANY	8:0	SAUDI ARABIA
05.06.	GERMANY	1:1	IRELAND
06.06.	CAMEROON	1:0	SAUDI ARABIA
11.06.	CAMEROON	0:2	GERMANY
11.06.	SAUDI ARABIA	0:3	IRELAND

PTS: GERMANY 7, IRELAND 5, CAMEROON 4, SAUDI ARABIA 0

GROUP F

DATE	TEAM	R	TEAM
02.06.	ENGLAND	1:1	SWEDEN
02.06.	ARGENTINA	1:0	NIGERIA
07.06.	SWEDEN	2:1	NIGERIA
07.06.	ARGENTINA	0:1	ENGLAND
12.06.	SWEDEN	1:1	ARGENTINA
12.06.	NIGERIA	0:0	ENGLAND

PTS: SWEDEN 5, ENGLAND 5, ARGENTINA 4, NIGERIA 1

GROUP G

DATE	TEAM	R	TEAM
03.06.	CROATIA	0:1	MEXICO
03.06.	ITALY	2:0	ECUADOR
08.06.	ITALY	1:2	CROATIA
09.06.	MEXICO	2:1	ECUADOR
13.06.	MEXICO	1:1	ITALY
13.06.	ECUADOR	1:0	CROATIA

PTS: MEXICO 7, ITALY 4, CROATIA 3, ECUADOR 3

GROUP H

DATE	TEAM	R	TEAM
04.06.	JAPAN	2:2	BELGIUM
05.06.	RUSSIA	2:0	TUNISIA
09.06.	JAPAN	1:0	RUSSIA
10.06.	TUNISIA	1:1	BELGIUM
14.06.	TUNISIA	0:2	JAPAN
14.06.	BELGIUM	3:2	RUSSIA

PTS: JAPAN 7, BELGIUM 5, RUSSIA 3, TUNISIA 1

ROUND OF 16

DATE	TEAM	R	TEAM
15.06.	GERMANY	1:0	PARAGUAY
15.06.	DENMARK	0:3	ENGLAND
16.06.	SWEDEN	1:2 E.T	SENEGAL
16.06.	SPAIN	1:1 E.T, 3:2 P.	IRELAND
17.06.	MEXICO	0:2	USA
17.06.	BRAZIL	2:0	BELGIUM
18.06.	JAPAN	0:1	TURKEY
18.06.	SOUTH KOREA	2:1 E.T	ITALY

QUARTER-FINALS

DATE	TEAM	R	TEAM
21.06.	ENGLAND	1:2	BRAZIL
21.06.	GERMANY	1:0	USA
22.06.	SPAIN	0:0 E.T, 3:5 P.	SOUTH KOREA
22.06.	SENEGAL	0:1	TURKEY

SEMIFINALS

DATE	TEAM	R	TEAM
25.06.	GERMANY	1:0	SOUTH KOREA
26.06.	BRAZIL	1:0	TURKEY

3RD PLACE

DATE	TEAM	R	TEAM
29.06	SOUTH KOREA	2:3	TURKEY

FINAL

DATE	TEAM	R	TEAM
30.06.	GERMANY	0:2	BRAZIL

CHAMPION: BRAZIL

TICKET 2002

QUALIFIED TEAMS

32 (FROM 198 CANDIDATES)

PLAYERS IN FIELD

581

FASTEST GOAL

11 SECONDS: HAKAN SÜKÜR (TURKEY–SOUTH KOREA)

TOP SCORERS

GOLDEN BOOT, 8 GOALS

RONALDO (BRAZIL)

SILVER BOOT, 5 GOALS

KLOSE (GERMANY), RIVALDO (BRAZIL)

BEST GOALKEEPER

OLIVER KAHN (GERMANY)

BEST YOUNG PLAYER

LANDON DONOVAN, 20 YEARS (USA)

PERIOD

31ST MAY, 2002–30TH JUNE, 2002

MATCHES

64

MOST MAN OF THE MATCH

RIVALDO (BRAZIL), 3

FAIR PLAY AWARD

BELGIUM

YELLOW CARDS

266 (Ø: 4.16 PER MATCH)

YELLOW-RED CARDS

6 (Ø: 0.09 PER MATCH)

RED CARDS

11 (Ø: 0.17 PER MATCH)

3 OR MORE GOALS IN A MATCH

3 GOALS: PAULETA (PORTUGAL–POLAND), KLOSE (GERMANY–SAUDI ARABIA)

ATTENDANCE

2,705,197 (Ø: 42,269 PER MATCH)

GOALS

161 (Ø: 2.52 PER MATCH)

OWN GOALS

4

MOST DANGEROUS TEAM

BRAZIL: 18 GOALS IN 7 MATCHES

BEST PLAYER

GOLDEN BALL

OLIVER KAHN (GERMANY)

SILVER BALL

RONALDO (BRAZIL)

BRONZE BALL

HONG MYUNG-BO (SOUTH KOREA)

PENALTIES

18: 13 SCORED, 5 MISSED

DREAM TEAM 2002

2006 GERMANY

ZIDANE HEAD BUTTED MATERAZZI IN THE FINAL

2006 GERMANY

The whole world was amazed at the World Cup which was celebrated in Germany (from June 9 to July 9), in spite of the violent reaction of the legendary player Zidane. Germans were happy. They were proud of their team and proud to host the World Cup.

The World Cup's slogan, "A time to make friends," expressed the German hospitality by televising the matches on big screens and on public buildings where people could enjoy the matches under the blazing sun. These kind gestures will always be remembered.

In the first stage, Germany won all three of their matches. Lukas Podolski, who was later confirmed as the best young player of the World Cup, scored the two decisive goals against Sweden in the round of sixteen. Argentina lost a World Cup penalty shoot-out for the first time and was eliminated from the competition, giving Die Mannschaft the victory. In that match—bafflingly—coach José Pékerman never brought a certain 19-year-old Lionel Messi off the bench, and later, goalkeeper Jens Lehmann relied on a "memory aid" to guess the four penalty kicks, saving two of them. Germany advanced to the semifinal against Italy, where they lost 2-0 in the last minutes of extra time. However, Germany beat Portugal 3-1 in the match for third place.

The round of sixteen between Portugal and the Netherlands was thrilling, especially because of the 16 bookings and four red cards. Brazilian player Ronaldo raced past Gerd Müller in the all-time World Cup scoring charts, taking his tally to 15 goals. France, helped by a remarkable Zidane performance, knocked out Brazil in the quarter-finals. France faced Italy in the final. The Italian defense was considered the best among all the World Cup teams, since they conceded only two goals. The match finished 1-1 after extra time. At this point, the superstar Zinedine Zidane overreacted to Marco Materazzi's provocation and headbutted him in the chest. Zizou received a red card and was sent off. Italy won the match in the penalty shoot-out.

Fabio Grosso, who had already been Germany's executioner, was also the one who scored the decisive penalty, taking him from being "Il Principe di Dortmund" (the Prince of Dortmund) to becoming "Il Re di Berlino" (the King of Berlin).

ZIDANE LEFT THE PITCH AFTER THE RED CARD.
THE SPECTATORS COULD NOT BELIEVE IT...

THE ACROBATIC MIROSLAV KLOSE WON THE GOLDEN BOOT AFTER SCORING 5 GOALS

SINCE 2006, RONALDO, WITH HIS 15 GOALS, BECAME THE HIGHEST SCORER IN THE WORLD CUP UNTIL THEN. THIS IS HIS FINAL GOAL; HE BAMBOOZLES THE GHANIAN GOALKEEPER RICHARD KINGSON

MICHAEL BALLACK, THE GERMAN CAPTAIN, ENTERS THE PITCH

THE PIECE OF PAPER, WHICH JENS LEHMANN READS BEFORE SAVING THE ARGENTINA PENALTY KICKS, CONTAINS INFORMATION ABOUT SOME ARGENTINE PLAYERS WHEN KICKING A PENALTY

OUCH!

WAYNE ROONEY PUTS AT RISK RICARDO CARVALHO´S FAMILY PLANS. CRISTIANO RONALDO, ROONEY´S TEAM MATE AT MANCHESTER UNITED, EXPLAINS TO THE REFEREE HOW AWFUL IT IS TO BE STAMPED ON THAT PART OF THE BODY, AND THE ENGLISH PLAYER IS SENT OFF.

RONALDO GIVES A WINK TO THE PORTUGUESE BENCH AS IF HE WERE SAYING: "WELL, WE GOT RID OF HIM"

ROBERTO CARLOS AND COMPANY GET DISTRACTED. THIERRY HENRY FINDS HIMSELF ONE ON ONE AND SCORES THE WINNER. FRANCE ADVANCES TO THE SEMIFINALS

ZIDANE

?!

DIDA

ZZZ

HENRY

ROBERTO CARLOS

2006 WORLD CHAMPIONS: ITALY.

TOP: GIANLUIGI BUFFON, MARCO MATERAZZI, LUCA TONI, FABIO GROSSO, FRANCESCO TOTTI. BOTTOM: GENNARO GATTUSO, ANDREA PIRLO, MAURC CAMORANESI, FABIO CANNAVARO, GIANLUCA ZAMBROTTA, SIMONE PERRO

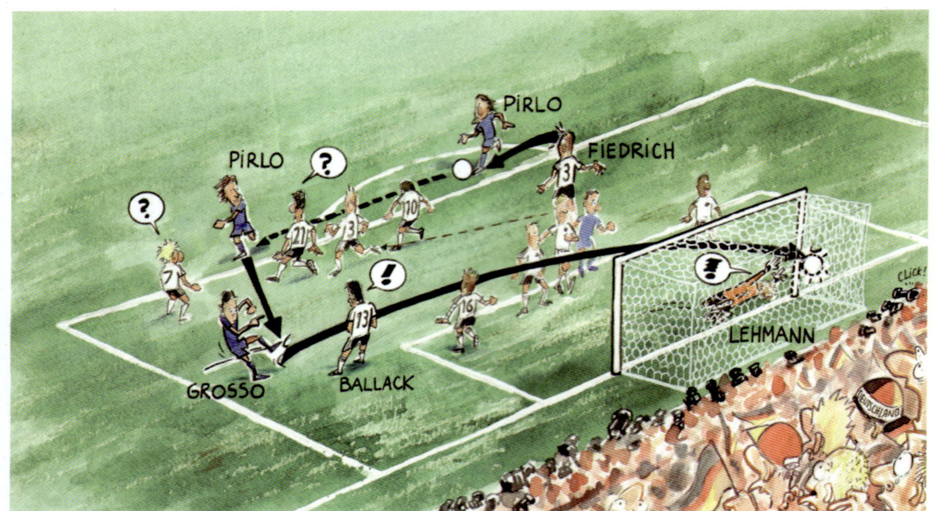

ITALY ELIMINATES THE HOST TEAM. IN THE 119TH MINUTE, GROSSO SCORES THE FIRST GOAL FOR ITALY

THE FINAL

9TH JULY, 2006

ITALIA 1:1 FRANCE (EXTRA-TIME)

PENALTIES: 5-3

OLYMPIASTADION, BERLIN
ATTENDANCE: 69,000
REFEREE: HORACIO ELIZONDO (ARGENTINA)

THE BALL USED FOR THE FINAL

COACH MARCELLO LIPPI LIFTS UP THE FOURTH WORLD CUP FOR ITALY

0:1
PENALTY. ZIDANE: OFF THE BAR AND IN
7TH MINUTE
ZIDANE 10
1:1
MATERAZZI HEADS HOME
19TH MINUTE
BARTHEZ 16
EXTRA-TIME
111TH MINUTE
THE MOST STUNNING MOMENT IN THE WORLD CUP: ZIDANE FINISHES HIS OUTSTANDING CAREER HEAD BUTTING MATERAZZI AND BEING SENT OFF IN THE FINAL
PENALTIES: TREZEGUET HITS THE CROSSBAR!
GROSSO ... GOOAAAAL !!!
THE VICTORY
ITALY WORLD CHAMPION!
-ACZEL-

2006 IN OVERVIEW

GROUP A

DATE	TEAM	R	TEAM
09.06.	GERMANY	4:2	COSTA RICA
09.06.	POLAND	0:2	ECUADOR
14.06.	GERMANY	1:0	POLAND
15.06.	ECUADOR	3:0	COSTA RICA
20.06.	ECUADOR	0:3	GERMANY
20.06.	COSTA RICA	1:2	POLAND

PTS: GERMANY 9, ECUADOR 6, POLAND 3, COSTA RICA 0

GROUP B

DATE	TEAM	R	TEAM
10.06.	ENGLAND	1:0	PARAGUAY
10.06.	TRINIDAD & TOBAGO	0:0	SWEDEN
15.06.	ENGLAND	2:0	TRINIDAD & TOBAGO
15.06.	SWEDEN	1:0	PARAGUAY
20.06.	SWEDEN	2:2	ENGLAND
20.06.	PARAGUAY	2:0	TRINIDAD & TOBAGO

PTS: ENGLAND 7, SWEDEN 5, PARAGUAY 3, TRINIDAD & TOBAGO 1

GROUP C

DATE	TEAM	R	TEAM
10.06.	ARGENTINA	2:1	IVORY COAST
11.06.	SERBIA & MONTEN.	0:1	NETHERLANDS
16.06.	ARGENTINA	6:0	SERBIA & MONTEN.
16.06.	NETHERLANDS	2:1	IVORY COAST
21.06.	NETHERLANDS	0:0	ARGENTINA
21.06.	ELFENBEINKÜSTE	3:2	SERBIA & MONTEN.

PTS: ARGENTINA 7, NL 7, IVORY COAST 3, SERBIA & MONTENEGRO 0

GROUP D

DATE	TEAM	R	TEAM
11.06.	MEXICO	3:1	IRAN
11.06.	ANGOLA	0:1	PORTUGAL
16.06.	MEXICO	0:0	ANGOLA
17.06.	PORTUGAL	2:0	IRAN
21.06.	PORTUGAL	2:1	MEXICO
21.06.	IRAN	1:1	ANGOLA

PTS: PORTUGAL 9, MEXICO 4, ANGOLA 2, IRAN 1

GROUP E

DATE	TEAM	R	TEAM
12.06.	ITALY	2:0	GHANA
12.06.	USA	0:3	CZECH REPUBLIC
17.06.	ITALY	1:1	USA
17.06.	CZECH REPUBLIC	0:2	GHANA
22.06.	CZECH REPUBLIC	0:2	ITALY
22.06.	GHANA	2:1	USA

PTS: ITALY 7, GHANA 6, CZECH REPUBLIC 3, USA 1

GROUP F

DATE	TEAM	R	TEAM
12.06.	AUSTRALIA	3:1	JAPAN
13.06.	BRAZIL	1:0	CROATIA
18.06.	BRAZIL	2:0	AUSTRALIA
18.06.	JAPAN	0:0	CROATIA
22.06.	JAPAN	1:4	BRAZIL
22.06.	CROATIA	2:2	AUSTRALIA

PTS: BRAZIL 9, AUSTRALIA 4, CROATIA 2, JAPAN 1

GROUP G

DATE	TEAM	R	TEAM
13.06.	FRANCE	0:0	SWITZERLAND
13.06.	SOUTH KOREA	2:1	TOGO
18.06.	FRANCE	1:1	SOUTH KOREA
19.06.	TOGO	0:2	SWITZERLAND
23.06.	TOGO	0:2	FRANCE
23.06.	SWITZERLAND	2:0	SOUTH KOREA

PTS: SWITZERLAND 7, FRANCE 5, SOUTH KOREA 4, TOGO 0

GROUP H

DATE	TEAM	R	TEAM
14.06.	SPAIN	4:0	UKRAINE
14.06.	TUNISIA	2:2	SAUDI ARABIA
19.06.	SPAIN	3:1	TUNISIA
19.06.	SAUDI ARABIA	0:4	UKRAINE
23.06.	SAUDI ARABIA	0:1	SPAIN
23.06.	UKRAINE	1:0	TUNISIA

PTS: SPAIN 9, UKRAINE 6, TUNISIA 1, SAUDI ARABIA 1

ROUND OF 16

DATE	TEAM	R	TEAM
24.06.	GERMANY	2:0	SWEDEN
24.06.	ARGENTINA	2:1 E.T	MEXICO
25.06.	ENGLAND	1:0	ECUADOR
25.06.	PORTUGAL	1:0	NETHERLANDS
26.06.	ITALY	1:0	AUSTRALIA
26.06.	SWITZERLAND	0:0 E.T, 0:3 P.	UKRAINE
27.06.	BRAZIL	3:0	GHANA
27.06.	SPAIN	1:3	FRANCE

3RD PLACE

DATE	TEAM	R	TEAM
08.07.	GERMANY	3:1	PORTUGAL

QUARTER-FINALS

DATE	TEAM	R	TEAM
30.06.	GERMANY	1:1 E.T, 4:2 P.	ARGENTINA
30.06.	ITALY	3:0	UKRAINE
01.07.	ENGLAND	0:0 E.T, 1:3 P.	PORTUGAL
01.07.	BRAZIL	0:1	FRANCE

SEMIFINALS

DATE	TEAM	R	TEAM
04.07.	GERMANY	0:2 E.T	ITALY
05.07.	PORTUGAL	0:1	FRANCE

FINAL

DATE	TEAM	R	TEAM
09.07.	ITALY	1:1 E.T, 5:3 P.	FRANCE

CHAMPION: ITALY

QUALIFIED TEAMS
32 (FROM 198 CANDIDATES)

PLAYERS IN FIELD
598

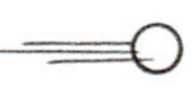

FASTEST GOAL
68 SECONDS: GYAN
(GHANA–CZECH REPUBLIC)

TOP SCORERS
GOLDEN BOOT, 5 GOALS
MIROSLAV KLOSE (GERMANY)
SILVER BOOT, 3 GOALS
HERNAN CRESPO (ARGENTINA)
BRONZE BOOT, 3 GOALS
RONALDO (BRAZIL)

BEST GOALKEEPER
GIANLUIGI BUFFON (ITALY)

BEST YOUNG PLAYER
LUKAS PODOLSKI,
21 YEARS (GERMANY)

PERIOD
9TH JUNE, 2006–9TH JULY, 2006

MATCHES
64

MOST MAN OF THE MATCH
ANDREA PIRLO (ITALY), 3

FAIR PLAY AWARD
BRAZIL UND SPAIN

YELLOW CARDS
326 (Ø: 5.09 PER MATCH)

YELLOW-RED CARDS
19 (Ø: 0.3 PER MATCH)

RED CARDS
9 (Ø: 0.14 PER MATCH)

3 OR MORE GOALS IN A MATCH
–

ATTENDANCE
3,359,439 (Ø: 52,491 PER MATCH)

GOALS
147 (Ø: 2.3 PER MATCH)

OWN GOALS
4

MOST DANGEROUS TEAM
GERMANY: 14 GOALS
IN 7 MATCHES

BEST PLAYER
GOLDEN BALL
ZINEDINE ZIDANE (FRANCE)
SILVER BALL
FABIO CANNAVARO (ITALY)BRONZE
BALL
ANDREA PIRLO (ITALY)

PENALTIES
16: 13 SCORED, 3 MISSED

DREAM TEAM 2006

SOUTH AFRICA

2010 SOUTH AFRICA

VUVUZELAS: THE SOUND THAT NEVER STOPPED

2010 SOUTH AFRICA

The vuvuzelas, which made an unbearable blast that seemed to be the buzz of millions of wasps, were, undoubtedly, the South African sound of the first World Cup held in Africa from June 11 to July 11, 2010, together with Shakira's Waka Waka, of course.

It was the first time that Serbia and the Slovak Republic added their names to the World Cup. The Slovak Republic's participation surprised everyone, since they eliminated Italy, the defending champion, 3-2 in the last match of the first stage.

France was also sent home in the first stage, as this was one of their worst World Cups in living memory. The German team, coached by Joachim Löw, got, once more, the best results with 16 goals. In the last sixteen, Germany played the classic game against England, and defeated them 4-1. Frank Lampard's shot hit the crossbar and bounced beyond the goal line. However, the referee did not give it. This was referred to as 'the revenge for Wembley'. For the first time, Diego Maradona coached Argentina, but they were humiliated (4-0) by Germany in the last eight. Two weeks later, Maradona left the national team.

For Uruguay, it was their best World Cup since 1970: they finished in third place in a tournament where striker Luis Suárez saved a ball destined for goal with his hands in the last minute, for which he was obviously sent off; Sebastián Abreu executed a "Panenka" on a decisive penalty (and scored it), and Diego Forlán was awarded the Best Player of the tournament.

The Netherlands once again dreamed of lifting an elusive trophy and defeated strong opponents along the way, but in the final, the new "Total Orange" ran into the "Red Fury." Spain, who had won the European Championship two years earlier, arrived as a favorite and did not falter. With the leadership of Andrés Iniesta—who also scored the winning goal in the 116th minute—alongside the marking of Sergio Ramos and Gerard Piqué, and the goals of David Villa, Spain triumphed 1-0 and celebrated as World Cup champions for the first time.

IN THE 116TH MINUTE, INIESTA SCORES THE WINNER

THE REVENGE FOR WEMBLEY 1966

LUiS SUÁREZ
UNFORGETTABLE HANDBALL iN THE LAST SECOND AGAiNST GHANA, KEEPS HiS TEAM ALiVE iN THE WORLD CUP

THE HANDS OF LUiS FABiANO

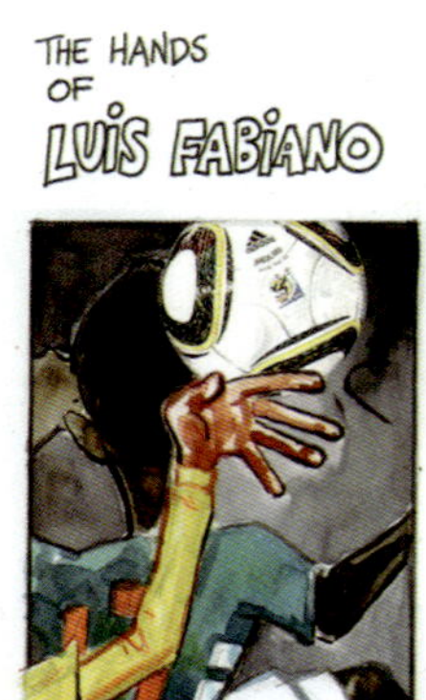

THE BRAZiLiAN PLAYER FABiANO HiTS THE BALL, FiRST WiTH HiS LEFT HAND AND THEN WiTH THE RiGHT ONE. THE REFEREE ASKED, "WiTH YOUR CHEST, RiGHT?" "YES, SURE!" "OK, i BELiEVE YOU"

STRIKE: THE FRENCH PLAYERS HAVE TROUBLES WITH THEIR COACH

DIEGO FORLÁN, THE WORLD CUP BEST PLAYER, WAS DECISIVE IN EACH MATCH

FINALLY, ANOTHER MÜLLER IN THE GERMAN TEAM! THOMAS MÜLLER BECAME THE WORLD CUP TOP SCORER WITH FIVE GOALS

IN THE SEMIFINAL AGAINST URUGUAY, THE DUTCH PLAYER SHOT FROM 40 YARDS AND ALMOST SCORED THE GOAL

XAVI DIRECTS THE CORNER KICK TO THE UNMARKED PUYOL WHO HEADS HOME THE WINNER IN THE SEMIFINAL AGAINST GERMANY

18
16
15
11
1
6
7
ACZEL

2010 WORLD CHAMPIONS: SPAIN.
TOP: PEDRO, BUSQUETS, SERGIO RAMOS, CAPDEVILA, PIQUÉ, XABI ALONSO. BOTTOM: CASILLAS, INIESTA, VILLA, XAVI, PUYOL

PAUL THE OCTOPUS PREDICTED TWELVE TIMES THE CORRECT OUTCOME

THE BALL USED IN THE FINAL

THE VICTORY'S ARCHITECT: VICENTE DEL BOSQUE, SPAIN COACH SINCE 2008

THE FINAL 11TH JULY, 2010

NETHERLANDS 0:1 SPAIN (EXTRA-TIME)

SOCCER CITY, JOHANNESBURG
ATTENDANCE: 84,490
REFEREE: HOWARD WEBB (ENGLAND)

BEFORE THE MATCH
JIMMY JUMP TRIES TO PUT A HAT ON WORLD CUP TROPHY
Jimmy Jump

28TH MINUTE
NIGEL DE JONG KUNG FU KICK ON XABI ALONSO. ONLY YELLOW CARD!

CASILLAS SAVES A ONE ON ONE AGAINST ROBBEN
62ND MINUTE

THE DUTCH NUMBER 3 IS SENT OFF
EXTRA-TIME
109TH MINUTE
HEITINGA
3

116TH MINUTE
FABREGAS ASSISTING INIESTA...

¡GOOOOOL!
DANI JARQUE SIEMPRE CON NOSOTROS

SPAIN CHAMPION!
-ACZEL-

2010 IN OVERVIEW

GROUP A

DATE	TEAM	R	TEAM
11.06.	SOUTH AFRICA	1:1	MEXICO
11.06.	URUGUAY	0:0	FRANCE
16.06.	SOUTH AFRICA	0:3	URUGUAY
17.06.	FRANCE	0:2	MEXICO
22.06.	MEXICO	0:1	URUGUAY
22.06.	FRANCE	1:2	SOUTH AFRICA

PTS: URUGUAY 7, MEXICO 4, SOUTH AFRICA 4, FRANCE 1

GROUP B

DATE	TEAM	R	TEAM
12.06.	SOUTH KOREA	2:0	GREECE
12.06.	ARGENTINA	1:0	NIGERIA
17.06.	ARGENTINA	4:1	SOUTH KOREA
17.06.	GREECE	2:1	NIGERIA
22.06.	NIGERIA	2:2	SOUTH KOREA
22.06.	GREECE	0:2	ARGENTINA

PTS: ARGENTINA 9, SOUTH KOREA 4, GREECE 3, NIGERIA 1

GROUP C

DATE	TEAM	R	TEAM
12.06.	ENGLAND	1:1	USA
13.06.	ALGERIA	0:1	SLOVENIA
18.06.	SLOVENIA	2:2	USA
18.06.	ENGLAND	0:0	ALGERIA
23.06.	USA	1:0	ALGERIA
23.06.	SLOVENIA	0:1	ENGLAND

PTS: USA 5, ENGLAND 5, SLOVENIA 4, ALGERIA 1

GROUP D

DATE	TEAM	R	TEAM
13.06.	SERBIA	0:1	GHANA
13.06.	GERMANY	4:0	AUSTRALIA
18.06.	GERMANY	0:1	SERBIA
19.06.	GHANA	1:1	AUSTRALIA
23.06.	AUSTRALIA	2:1	SERBIA
23.06.	GHANA	0:1	GERMANY

PTS: GERMANY 6, GHANA 4, AUSTRALIA 4, SERBIA 3

GROUP E

DATE	TEAM	R	TEAM
14.06.	NETHERLANDS	2:0	DENMARK
14.06.	JAPAN	1:0	CAMEROON
19.06.	NETHERLANDS	1:0	JAPAN
19.06.	CAMEROON	1:2	DENMARK
24.06.	DENMARK	1:3	JAPAN
24.06.	CAMEROON	1:2	NETHERLANDS

PTS: NETHERLANDS 9, JAPAN 6, DENMARK 3, CAMEROON 0

GROUP F

DATE	TEAM	R	TEAM
14.06.	ITALY	1:1	PARAGUAY
15.06.	NEW ZEALAND	1:1	SLOVAKIA
20.06.	SLOVAKIA	0:2	PARAGUAY
20.06.	ITALY	1:1	NEW ZEALAND
24.06.	SLOVAKIA	3:2	ITALY
24.06.	PARAGUAY	0:0	NEW ZEALAND

PTS: PARAGUAY 5, SLOVAKIA 4, NEW ZEALAND 3, ITALY 2

GROUP G

DATE	TEAM	R	TEAM
15.06.	IVORY COAST	0:0	PORTUGAL
15.06.	BRAZIL	2:1	NORTH KOREA
20.06.	BRAZIL	3:1	IVORY COAST
21.06.	PORTUGAL	7:0	NORTH KOREA
25.06.	PORTUGAL	0:0	BRAZIL
25.06.	NORTH KOREA	0:3	IVORY COAST

PTS: BRAZIL 7, PORTUGAL 5, IVORY COAST 4, NORTH KOREA 0

GROUP H

DATE	TEAM	R	TEAM
16.06.	HONDURAS	0:1	CHILE
16.06.	SPAIN	0:1	SWITZERLAND
21.06.	CHILE	1:0	SWITZERLAND
21.06.	SPAIN	2:0	HONDURAS
25.06.	CHILE	1:2	SPAIN
25.06.	SWITZERLAND	0:0	HONDURAS

PTS: SPAIN 6, CHILE 6, SWITZERLAND 4, HONDURAS 1

ROUND OF 16

DATE	TEAM	R	TEAM
26.06.	URUGUAY	2:1	SOUTH KOREA
26.06.	USA	1:2 E.T	GHANA
27.06.	GERMANY	4:1	ENGLAND
27.06.	ARGENTINA	3:1	MEXICO
28.06.	NETHERLANDS	2:1	SLOVAKIA
28.06.	BRAZIL	3:0	CHILE
29.06.	PARAGUAY	0:0 E.T, 5:3 P.	JAPAN
29.06.	SPAIN	1:0	PORTUGAL

QUARTER-FINALS

DATE	TEAM	R	TEAM
02.07.	NETHERLANDS	2:1	BRAZIL
02.07.	URUGUAY	1:1 E.T, 4:2 P.	GHANA
03.07.	ARGENTINA	0:4	GERMANY
03.07.	PARAGUAY	0:1	SPAIN

SEMIFINALS

DATE	TEAM	R	TEAM
06.07.	URUGUAY	2:3	NETHERLANDS
07.07.	GERMANY	0:1	SPAIN

3RD PLACE

DATE	TEAM	R	TEAM
10.07.	URUGUAY	2:3	GERMANY

FINAL

DATE	TEAM	R	TEAM
11.07.	NETHERLANDS	0:1 E.T	SPAIN

CHAMPION:
SPAIN

TICKET 2010

QUALIFIED TEAMS
32 (FROM 206 CANDIDATES)

PLAYERS IN FIELD
599

FASTEST GOAL
2 MINUTES: THOMAS MÜLLER
(GERMANY–ARGENTINA)

TOP SCORERS
GOLDEN BOOT, 5 GOALS
THOMAS MÜLLER (GERMANY)
SILVER BOOT, 5 GOALS
DAVID VILLA (SPAIN)
BRONZE BOOT, 5 GOALS
WESLEY SNEIJDER (NETHERLANDS)

BEST GOALKEEPER
IKER CASILLAS (SPAIN)

BEST YOUNG PLAYER
THOMAS MÜLLER,
20 YEARS (GERMANY)

PERIOD
11TH JUNE, 2010–11TH JULY, 2010

MATCHES
64

MOST MAN OF THE MATCH
WESLEY SNEIJDER
(NETHERLANDS), 4

FAIR PLAY AWARD
SPAIN

YELLOW CARDS
261 (Ø: 4.08 PER MATCH)

YELLOW-RED CARDS
8 (Ø: 0.13 PER MATCH)

RED CARDS
9 (Ø: 0.14 PER MATCH)

3 OR MORE GOALS IN A MATCH
3 GOALS: GONZALO HIGUAÍN
ARGENTINA – SOUTH KOREA

ATTENDANCE
3,178,856 (Ø: 49,670 PER MATCH)

GOALS
145 (Ø: 2.27 PER MATCH)

OWN GOALS
2

MOST DANGEROUS TEAM
GERMANY: 16 GOALS
IN 7 MATCHES

BEST PLAYER
GOLDEN BALL
DIEGO FORLÁN (URUGUAY)
SILVER BALL
WESLEY SNEIJDER (NETHERLANDS)
BRONZE BALL
DAVID VILLA (SPAIN)

PENALTIES
15: 9 SCORED,
6 MISSED

DREAM TEAM 2010

ACZEL

2014 BRAZIL

THE GHOST OF 1950 'MARACANAZO' ADDED ANOTHER FELLOW IN 2014: 'MINEIRAZO'. GERMANY DANCES SAMBA WITH BRAZIL AND OFFERS AN UNFORGETTABLE GOAL SHOW

2014 BRAZIL

Finally, World Champions! After winning the tournament in Brazil (from June 12 to July 13), the German National team of Joachim Löw accomplished a mission that had started with the team development in 2004. After reaching the semifinals in World Cups and European Tournaments since 2002, the fourth victory after 1954, 1974 and 1990 seemed to be the perfect end.

32 teams qualified for the Cup. Bosnia and Herzegovina participated for the first time. In this tournament a total of 171 goals were scored, the highest-scoring in history, along with France 1998. Among the most memorable moments was Robin van Persie's goal, a diving header that leveled the match and opened the way for the Netherlands' 5–1 rout of the defending champions Spain.

On the other hand, the great Uruguayan forward Luis Suárez was punished for biting Giorgio Chiellini from Italy on the shoulder, and because he had already committed the same offence before. He was suspended for nine matches and banned for four months from any soccer-related activity. Uruguay was out in the second round, when the Colombian James Rodríguez, with a dream volley, scored the best goal of the Cup, apart from earning the Golden Boot with six goals.

Argentina advanced with Lionel Messi leading a young team eager to win another title. Switzerland, Belgium, and the Netherlands could not stop the Albiceleste, who reached the final again after 24 years.

Manuel Neuer reinvented the sweeper role. The German goalkeeper, with 19 situations in which he left the penalty area, helped his team to win 2-1 in the second stage against Algeria. Is it possible that in the future goalkeepers will not just prevent the opposition from scoring? Neuer may be the first modern, complete sweeper-keeper. For his performance, he won the Best FIFA Goalkeeper Award.

Brazil, who were favorites to win the Cup, had a terrible time during this tournament. In the quarter-finals, superstar Neymar fractured a vertebra in his spine when he was kneed in the back by Juan Zuñiga in a challenge that went unpunished. Brazil lost their best striker, but the worst was yet to come. The semifinal against Germany was a huge humiliation for

YESSSSS! GOOAALLL!

1-0 GÖTZE FIGHTS THE FINAL BATTLE AGAINST ARGENTINA AND SCORES THE WINNER IN MINUTE 113

Brazilian soccer. They were thrashed by Germany 1-7. Five goals fell in an 18-minute span in the first half (four of them in just six minutes), in what looked like a match between professionals and amateurs. The entire world could not believe what it was seeing, and the whole nation wept.

And so, Argentina and Germany met for the third time in a World Cup final, with one win each. On Sunday, July 13th, 2014, Löw's players faced an opponent who, despite being superior for much of the match, failed to convert the chances they created. Everything seemed headed for a penalty shoot-out, but in the 113th minute, after a brilliant pass from André Schürrle, Mario Götze would seal the victory for Germany, which became the first European team to win the World Cup in the Americas.

VAN PERSIE´S DIVING HEADER
FLYING LIKE A SOCCER SUPERHERO: ROBIN VAN PERSIE EQUALIZES WITH SPAIN 1-1. AN ICONIC SUPER GOAL FROM THIS HISTORIC MATCH. NEVER BEFORE HAD A CHAMPION TEAM LOST WITH SUCH A DIFFERENCE IN THE NEXT EDITION. RESULT: 1-5. THE NETHERLANDS TOOK THE PERFECT REVENGE FOR THE 2010 FINAL!

SUAREZ SANK HIS TEETH ON CHIELLINI´S SHOULDER. HE WAS LATER SUSPENDED AND BANNED FROM SPORT EVENTS FOR A PERIOD OF TIME, APART FROM PAYING A LARGE SUM OF MONEY AS A FINE, IMPOSED FOR HAVING REPEATED THE OFFENCE

BRAZILIAN STAR: NEYMAR JR.

FOUR STRONG NATIONAL TEAMS DO NOT QUALIFY FOR THE ROUND OF 16. THIS FACT DRAWS THE ATTENTION OF EVERYONE

'FAVELAS'

AS RONALDO AND RONALDINHO SAID, BRAZIL, HOST OF CREATIVE SOCCER, TECHNICALLY BRILLIANT, HAS TO FOLLOW GERMANY'S EXAMPLE ON EDUCATION AND TRAINING OF YOUNG TALENTS, AND TRAVEL FROM THE 'FAVELAS' TO THE TOP OF WORLD SOCCER AGAIN

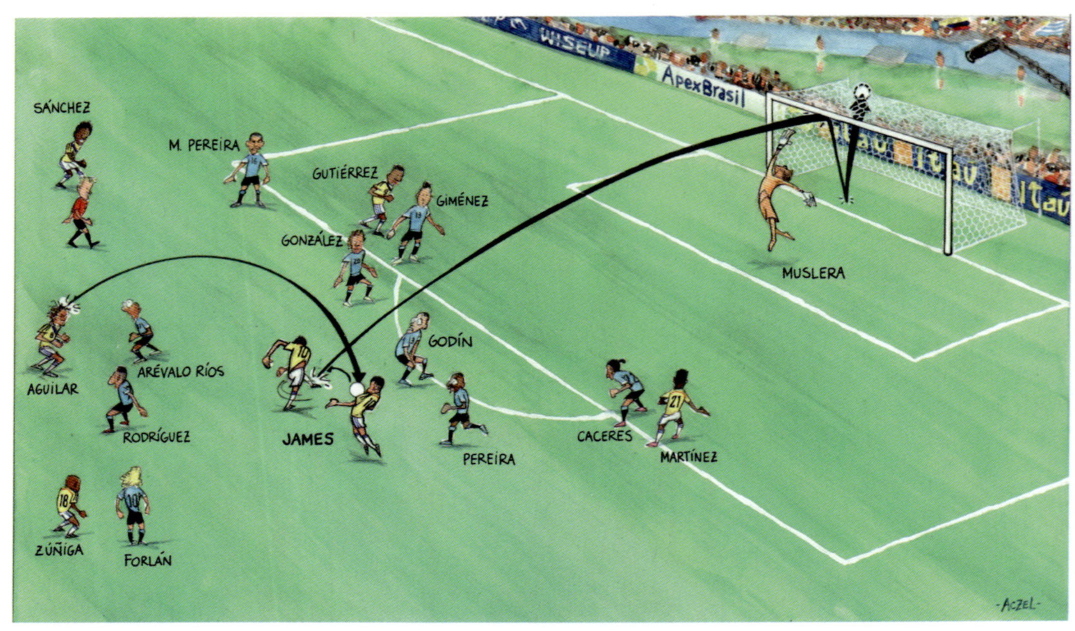

AT THE AGE OF 22, COLOMBIAN JAMES RODRÍGUEZ BECAME AN INTERNATIONAL STAR, AND WITH SIX GOALS, THE TOP SCORER OF THE CUP. THIS WAS HIS BEST GOAL AGAINST URUGUAY

SPRAY (OR SHAVING FOAM) IS USED BY REFEREES FOR THE FIRST TIME.

GOAL-LINE TECHNOLOGY ALSO FOR THE FIRST TIME

BRYAN RUIZ, CAPTAIN OF 'LOS TICOS'. THE NATIONAL TEAM OF COSTA RICA WAS FIRST IN THEIR GROUP LEAVING ITALY, URUGUAY AND ENGLAND BEHIND. AFTER BEATING GREECE, THEY WERE DEFEATED BY THE NETHERLANDS ON PENALTIES

MEROUANE FELLAINI (BELGIUM).
FLAMBOYANT HAIRSTYLE

36-YEAR-OLD KLOSE BROKE RONALDO´S RECORD.
HE WAS THE LEADING GOAL SCORER WITH 16 GOALS IN WORLD CUPS. HE SCORED 5 GOALS IN 2002, 5 IN 2006, 4 IN 2010 AND 2 GOALS IN 2014

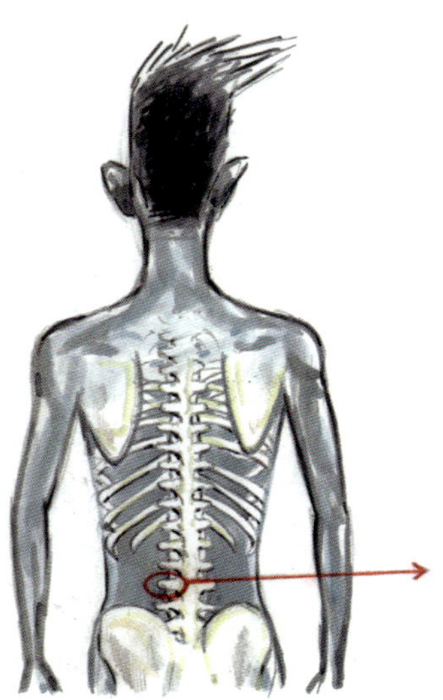

NEYMAR WAS BRAZIL´S HOPE. UNFORTUNATELY, HE WAS INJURED IN HIS BACK BY COLOMBIAN PLAYER ZUÑIGA WHO HIT THE BRAZIL STRIKER WITH A BRUTAL KNEE TO THE BACK. DIAGNOSIS: FRACTURE OF THE THIRD LUMBAR VERTEBRA

13
5
2014

2014 WORLD CHAMPIONS: GERMANY.
TOP: MANUEL NEUER, BENEDIKT HÖWEDES, SAMI KHEDIRA,
JÉRÔME BOATENG, MIROSLAV KLOSE. BOTTOM: PHILIPP LA

JOACHIM LÖW,
COACH OF A GOLDEN GENERATION

DISCIPLINE, TEAM SPIRIT AND THE NEVER GIVE UP SPIRIT ALWAYS PAYS!

THE BALL USED IN THE FINAL

THE FINAL 13TH JULY, 2014

GERMANY 1:0 ARGENTINA (EXTRA-TIME)

MARACANÃ STADIUM, RIO DE JANEIRO
ATTENDANCE: 74,738
REFEREE: NICOLA RIZZOLI (ITALY)

CONSOLATION PRIZE: LIONEL MESSI WON THE GOLDEN BALL FOR THE BEST PLAYER OF THE TOURNAMENT. HE WOULD OBVIOUSLY HAVE PREFERRED TO WIN THE CUP

BEFORE KICK-OFF

TWO BIG LITTLE ONES GREET EACH OTHER

CLATTERED BY GARAY! KRAMER VERY CONFUSED CAN'T CONTINUE

17TH MINUTE

21ST MINUTE

HIGUAIN!!!!......... WHAT A MISS!

30TH MINUTE

45TH MINUTE

57TH MINUTE

EXTRA-TIME

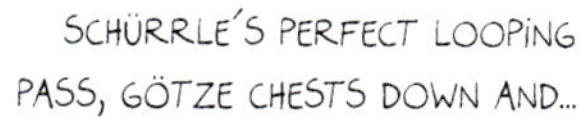

GOOAAL!

113TH MINUTE

2014 IN OVERVIEW

GROUP A

DATE	TEAM	R	TEAM
12.06.	BRAZIL	3:1	CROATIA
13.06.	MEXICO	1:0	CAMEROON
17.06.	BRAZIL	0:0	MEXICO
18.06.	CAMEROON	0:4	CROATIA
23.06.	CAMEROON	1:4	BRAZIL
23.06.	CROATIA	1:3	MEXICO

PTS: BRAZIL 7, MEXICO 7, CROATIA 3, CAMEROON 0

GROUP B

DATE	TEAM	R	TEAM
13.06.	SPAIN	1:5	NETHERLANDS
13.06.	CHILE	3:1	AUSTRALIA
18.06.	AUSTRALIA	2:3	NETHERLANDS
18.06.	SPAIN	0:2	CHILE
23.06.	AUSTRALIA	0:3	SPAIN
23.06.	NETHERLANDS	2:0	CHILE

PTS: NETHERLANDS 9, CHILE 6, SPAIN 3, AUSTRALIA 0

GROUP C

DATE	TEAM	R	TEAM
14.06.	COLOMBIA	3:0	GREECE
14.06.	IVORY COAST	2:1	JAPAN
19.06.	COLOMBIA	2:2	IVORY COAST
19.06.	JAPAN	0:0	GREECE
24.06.	JAPAN	1:4	COLOMBIA
24.06.	GREECE	2:1	IVORY COAST

PTS: COLOMBIA 9, GREECE 4, IVORY COAST 3, JAPAN 1

GROUP D

DATE	TEAM	R	TEAM
14.06.	URUGUAY	1:3	COSTA RICA
14.06.	ENGLAND	1:2	ITALY
19.06.	URUGUAY	2:1	ENGLAND
20.06.	ITALY	0:1	COSTA RICA
24.06.	ITALY	0:1	URUGUAY
24.06.	COSTA RICA	0:0	ENGLAND

PTS: COSTA RICA 7, URUGUAY 6, ITALY 3, ENGLAND 1

GROUP E

DATE	TEAM	R	TEAM
15.06.	SWITZERLAND	2:1	ECUADOR
15.06.	FRANCE	3:0	HONDURAS
20.06.	SWITZERLAND	2:5	FRANCE
20.06.	HONDURAS	1:2	ECUADOR
25.06.	HONDURAS	0:3	SWITZERLAND
25.06.	ECUADOR	0:0	FRANCE

PTS: FRANCE 7, SWITZERLAND 6, ECUADOR 4, HONDURAS 0

GROUP F

DATE	TEAM	R	TEAM
15.06.	ARGENTINA	2:1	BOSN. & HERZEGOV.
16.06.	IRAN	0:0	NIGERIA
21.06.	ARGENTINA	1:0	IRAN
21.06.	NIGERIA	1:0	BOSN. & HERZEGOV.
25.06.	NIGERIA	2:3	ARGENTINA
25.06.	BOSN. & HERZEGOV.	3:1	IRAN

PTS: ARGENTINA 9, NIGERIA 4, BOSN. & HERZEGOV. 3, IRAN 1

GROUP G

DATE	TEAM	R	TEAM
16.06.	GERMANY	4:0	PORTUGAL
16.06.	GHANA	1:2	USA
21.06.	GERMANY	2:2	GHANA
22.06.	USA	2:2	PORTUGAL
26.06.	USA	0:1	GERMANY
26.06.	PORTUGAL	2:1	GHANA

PTS: GERMANY 7, USA 4, PORTUGAL 4, GHANA 1

GROUP H

DATE	TEAM	R	TEAM
17.06.	BELGIUM	2:1	ALGERIA
17.06.	RUSSIA	1:1	SOUTH KOREA
22.06.	BELGIUM	1:0	RUSSIA
22.06.	SOUTH KOREA	2:4	ALGERIA
26.06.	SOUTH KOREA	0:1	BELGIUM
26.06.	ALGERIA	1:1	RUSSIA

PTS: BELGIUM 9, ALGERIA 4, RUSSIA 2, SOUTH KOREA 1

ROUND OF 16

DATE	TEAM	R	TEAM
28.06.	BRAZIL	1:1 E.T., 3:2 P.	CHILE
28.06.	COLOMBIA	2:0	URUGUAY
29.06.	NETHERLANDS	2:1	MEXICO
29.06.	COSTA RICA	1:1 E.T., 5:3 P.	GREECE
30.06.	FRANCE	2:0	NIGERIA
30.06.	GERMANY	2:1 E.T.	ALGERIA
01.07.	ARGENTINA	1:0 E.T.	SWITZERLAND
01.07.	BELGIUM	2:1 E.T.	USA

QUARTER-FINALS

DATE	TEAM	R	TEAM
04.07.	FRANCE	0:1	GERMANY
04.07.	BRAZIL	2:1	COLOMBIA
05.07.	ARGENTINA	1:0	BELGIUM
05.07.	NETHERLANDS	0:0 E.T., 4:3 P.	COSTA RICA

SEMIFINALS

DATE	TEAM	R	TEAM
08.07.	BRAZIL	1:7	GERMANY
09.07.	NETHERLANDS	0:0 E.T., 2:4 P.	ARGENTINA

3RD PLACE

DATE	TEAM	R	TEAM
12.07.	BRAZIL	0:3	NETHERLANDS

FINAL

DATE	TEAM	R	TEAM
13.07.	GERMANY	1:0 E.T.	ARGENTINA

CHAMPION: GERMANY

TICKET 2014

QUALIFIED TEAMS
32 (FROM 204 CANDIDATES)

PLAYERS IN FIELD
593

FASTEST GOAL
29 SECONDS: CLINT DEMPSEY (USA–GHANA)

TOP SCORERS
GOLDEN BOOT, 6 GOALS
JAMES RODRÍGUEZ (COLOMBIA)
SILVER BOOT, 5 GOALS
THOMAS MÜLLER (GERMANY)
BRONZE BOOT, 4 GOALS
NEYMAR (BRAZIL)

BEST GOALKEEPER
MANUEL NEUER (GERMANY)

BEST YOUNG PLAYER
PAUL POGBA,
21 YEARS (FRANCE)

PERIOD
12TH JUNE, 2014–13TH JULY, 2014

MATCHES
64

MOST MAN OF THE MATCH
LIONEL MESSI (ARGENTINA), 4

FAIR-PLAY AWARD
COLOMBIA

YELLOW CARDS
181 (Ø: 2.83 PER MATCH)

YELLOW-RED CARDS
3 (Ø: 0.05 PER MATCH)

RED CARDS
7 (Ø: 0.11 PER MATCH)

3 OR MORE GOALS IN A MATCH
3 GOALS: XHERDAN SHAQIRI (SWITZERLAND– HONDURAS), THOMAS MÜLLER (GERMANY–PORTUGAL)

ATTENDANCE
3,429,873 (Ø: 53.592 PER MATCH)

GOALS
171 (Ø: 2.67 PER MATCH)

OWN GOALS
5

MOST DANGEROUS TEAM
GERMANY: 18 GOALS IN 7 MATCHES

BEST PLAYER
GOLDEN BALL
LIONEL MESSI (ARGENTINA)
SILVER BALL
THOMAS MÜLLER (GERMANY)
BRONZE BALL
ARJEN ROBBEN (NETHERLANDS)

PENALTIES
13: 12 SCORED,
1 MISSED

DREAM TEAM 2014

VROAAA

-ACZEL-

2018 RUSSIA

19-YEAR-OLD MBAPPÉ, AS FAST AS A TORNADO. ACHIEVED THE AVERAGE SPEED OF USAIN BOLT: 23.35 MPH. HE FLEW PAST THE ARGENTINE PLAYERS.

2018 RUSSIA

Germany defending the title? Instead, it was a World Cup for the younger generation and for pragmatic soccer. France, Croatia and Belgium showed some great soccer moments. A tournament full of fallen favorites, surprises, the debut of the VAR and last-minute goals. This edition of the event was held from June 14 to July 15, 2018, marking the eleventh time it was held in Europe and the first in Eastern Europe.

The big disappointment was Germany, who were eliminated in the group stage in last place. So Pelé's Brazil remained the last successful team to defend its title.

Many other favorites also fell. Italy and the Netherlands did not even qualify. Spain with Ramos, Portugal with Cristiano Ronaldo and Argentina with Messi only made it to the round of 16; Brazil with Neymar and Uruguay with Suárez reached the quarterfinals. Neymar was more about the drama—falling on the ground—than concentrating on the game. In the round of 16, Argentina played what was the most spectacular and dynamic match of the World Cup against those who would become champions—France. "Les Bleus" won 4-3.

The African national teams didn't do well either. Egypt, Senegal, Tunisia, Morocco and Nigeria all failed to make it out of the group stage, leaving Africa without representation in the knockout stages for the first time since 1982. Overall, there had never been so many tight matches, often resulting in agonizing last-minute goals. There were four penalty shoot-outs, and 40% of all goals came from free kicks, corner kicks or penalties.

From the semifinals onward, the championship became purely European, consolidating the region's supremacy. The final four teams were England, Belgium, the surprising Croatia and France. Coach Didier Deschamps made his team play a counterattacking style, with quick changes from defense to attack, combined with dead ball moves. Kylian Mbappé was the perfect player for that: athletic, a miracle in speed and also sure to score. At 19, he became the youngest goal scorer in a World Cup final since Pelé. Winning the highest title in soccer at such a young age hinted at his great career. He embodied the new and modern face of soccer.

PAVARD (FRANCE) CUTS THE BALL WITH HIS RIGHT FOOT. THE BALL FLIES INTO THE LONG CORNER WITH WONDERFUL EFFECT, BEATING ARMANI (ARGENTINA). THE BEST GOAL OF THE WORLD CUP.

VAR WAS USED FOR THE FIRST TIME IN A WORLD CUP

ELIMINATED TOO SOON. TWO SUPER-STARS: MESSI AND CR7.

GERMANY'S WORST WORLD CUP PERFORMANCE. ELIMINATED IN THE GROUP STAGE, THE DEFENDING WORLD CHAMPIONS LEFT BEHIND A DEPLORABLE IMAGE.

SCORER HARRY KANE (6 GOALS)

CLEARLY, THE MOST RIDICULOUS AND FUNNY GOAL CELEBRATION OF THE WORLD CUP BELONGED TO BELGIAN BATSHUAYI. HE WANTED TO CELEBRATE HIS TEAM'S GOAL BY KICKING THE BALL BACK INTO THE BOTTOM OF THE NET, BUT HE DID NOT TAKE INTO ACCOUNT THE GOALPOST, WHICH BOUNCED THE BALL STRAIGHT INTO HIS FACE.

SHAQIRI (SWITZERLAND) AND CAVANI (URUGUAY) REACH THE QUARTERFINALS

MODRIĆ (CROATIA) WAS VOTED THE BEST WORLD CUP PLAYER. MBAPPÉ (FRANCE) WAS CHOSEN THE BEST YOUNG PLAYER.

NEYMAR WAS HARSHLY CRITICIZED FOR HIS DRAMATIC EXAGGERATIONS

IT'S NO JOKE: ENGLAND WON ON PENALTIES. THE CURSE WAS BROKEN.

RUSSIA, THE HOSTS, MOVED INTO THE QUARTERFINALS FOLLOWING A PENALTY SHOOT-OUT VICTORY OVER SPAIN

BELGIUM ELIMINATED BRAZIL. FOR THE FIRST TIME SINCE 1986, THE "RED DEVILS" REACHED THE SEMIFINALS. WORTH WATCHING: MIDFIELDER KEVIN DE BRUYNE HIT A BRILLIANT SHOT FROM THE RIGHT CORNER OF THE PENALTY AREA. HAZARD, LUKAKU AND DE BRUYNE WERE THE BEST ATTACKING TRIO OF THE WORLD CUP.

(ABOVE) CROATIA KICKED OUT THE TOURNAMENT HOSTS ON PENALTIES. (BELOW) CROATIA ELIMINATED ENGLAND AND REACHED THE WORLD CUP FINAL FOR THE FIRST TIME IN SOCCER HISTORY.

COUPE DU MONDE
DE LA RUSSIE 2018
FINALE
15 JUILLET 2018
MOSCOU

2018 WORLD CHAMPIONS: FRANCE.
TOP: PAUL POGBA, SAMUEL UMTITI, LUCAS HERNÁNDEZ, RAPH
OLIVIER GIROUD, HUGO LLORIS. BOTTOM: ANTOINE GRIEZMA
MATUIDI, BENJAMIN PAVARD, N'GOLO KANTÉ, KYLIAN MBAPPÉ

UMTITI TOOK FRANCE TO THE FINAL

THE BALL USED IN THE FINAL

THE FINAL 15TH JULY, 2018

FRANCE 4:2 CROATIA

LUZHNIKI OLYMPIC STADIUM, MOSCOW
ATTENDANCE: 78,011
REFEREE: NÉSTOR PITANA (ARGENTINA)

FRANCE'S COACH DIDIER DESCHAMPS IS THE THIRD PLAYER, AFTER ZAGALLO AND BECKENBAUER, TO WIN A WORLD CUP AS BOTH A PLAYER AND A COACH

WITH A POSITIVE,
RELAXED
ATTITUDE
AND HEALTHY
SELF-CONFIDENCE,
FRANCE
GOT ITS
SECOND STAR

2018 IN OVERVIEW

GROUP A

DATE	TEAM	R	TEAM
14.06.	RUSSIA	5:0	SAUDI ARABIA
15.06.	EGYPT	0:1	URUGUAY
19.06.	RUSSIA	3:1	EGYPT
20.06.	URUGUAY	1:0	SAUDI ARABIA
25.06.	URUGUAY	3:0	RUSSIA
25.06.	SAUDI ARABIA	2:1	EGYPT

PTS: URUGUAY 9, RUSSIA 6, SAUDI ARABIA 3, EGYPT 0

GROUP B

DATE	TEAM	R	TEAM
15.06.	MOROCCO	0:1	IRAN
15.06.	PORTUGAL	3:3	SPAIN
20.06.	PORTUGAL	1:0	MOROCCO
20.06.	IRAN	0:1	SPAIN
25.06.	IRAN	1:1	PORTUGAL
25.06.	SPAIN	2:2	MOROCCO

PTS: SPAIN 5, PORTUGAL 5, IRAN 4, MOROCCO 1

GROUP C

DATE	TEAM	R	TEAM
16.06.	FRANCE	2:1	AUSTRALIA
16.06.	PERU	0:1	DENMARK
21.06.	DENMARK	1:1	AUSTRALIA
21.06.	FRANCE	1:0	PERU
26.06.	DENMARK	0:0	FRANCE
26.06.	AUSTRALIA	0:2	PERU

PTS: FRANCE 7, DENMARK 5, PERU 3, AUSTRALIA 1

GROUP D

DATE	TEAM	R	TEAM
16.06.	ARGENTINA	1:1	ICELAND
16.06.	CROATIA	2:0	NIGERIA
21.06.	ARGENTINA	0:3	CROATIA
22.06.	NIGERIA	2:0	ICELAND
26.06.	NIGERIA	1:2	ARGENTINA
26.06.	ICELAND	1:2	CROATIA

PTS: CROATIA 9, ARGENTINA 4, NIGERIA 3, ICELAND 1

GROUP E

DATE	TEAM	R	TEAM
17.06.	COSTA RICA	0:1	SERBIA
17.06.	BRAZIL	1:1	SWITZERLAND
22.06.	BRAZIL	2:0	COSTA RICA
22.06.	SERBIA	1:2	SWITZERLAND
27.06.	SERBIA	0:2	BRAZIL
27.06.	SWITZERLAND	2:2	COSTA RICA

PTS: BRAZIL 7, SWITZERLAND 5, SERBIA 3, COSTA RICA 1

GROUP F

DATE	TEAM	R	TEAM
17.06.	GERMANY	0:1	MEXICO
18.06.	SWEDEN	1:0	SOUTH KOREA
23.06.	SOUTH KOREA	1:2	MEXICO
23.06.	GERMANY	2:1	SWEDEN
27.06.	SOUTH KOREA	2:0	GERMANY
27.06.	MEXICO	0:3	SWEDEN

PTS: SWEDEN 6, MEXICO 6, SOUTH KOREA 3, GERMANY 3

GROUP G

DATE	TEAM	R	TEAM
18.06.	BELGIUM	3:0	PANAMA
18.06.	TUNISIA	1:2	ENGLAND
23.06.	BELGIUM	5:2	TUNISIA
24.06.	ENGLAND	6:1	PANAMA
28.06.	ENGLAND	0:1	BELGIUM
28.06.	PANAMA	1:2	TUNISIA

PTS: BELGIUM 9, ENGLAND 6, TUNISIA 3, PANAMA 0

GROUP H

DATE	TEAM	R	TEAM
19.06.	COLOMBIA	1:2	JAPAN
19.06.	POLAND	1:2	SENEGAL
24.06.	JAPAN	2:2	SENEGAL
24.06.	POLAND	0:3	COLOMBIA
28.06.	JAPAN	0:1	POLAND
28.06.	SENEGAL	0:1	COLOMBIA

PTS: COLOMBIA 6, JAPAN 4, SENEGAL 4, POLAND 3

ROUND OF 16

DATE	TEAM	R	TEAM
30.06.	FRANCE	4:3	ARGENTINA
30.06.	URUGUAY	2:1	PORTUGAL
01.07.	SPAIN	1:1 E.T., 3:4 P.	RUSSIA
01.07.	CROATIA	1:1 E.T., 3:2 P.	DENMARK
02.07.	BRAZIL	2:0	MEXICO
02.07.	BELGIUM	3:2	JAPAN
03.07.	SWEDEN	1:0	SWITZERLAND
03.07.	COLOMBIA	1:1 E.T., 3:4 P.	ENGLAND

QUARTER-FINALS

DATE	TEAM	R	TEAM
06.07.	URUGUAY	0:2	FRANCE
06.07.	BRAZIL	1:2	BELGIUM
07.07.	SWEDEN	0:2	ENGLAND
07.07.	RUSSIA	2:2 E.T., 3:4 P.	CROATIA

SEMIFINALS

DATE	TEAM	R	TEAM
10.07.	FRANCE	1:0	BELGIUM
11.07.	CROATIA	2:1 E.T.	ENGLAND

3RD PLACE

DATE	TEAM	R	TEAM
14.07.	BELGIUM	2:0	ENGLAND

FINAL

DATE	TEAM	R	TEAM
15.07.	FRANCE	4:2	CROATIA

CHAMPION: FRANCE

TICKET 2018

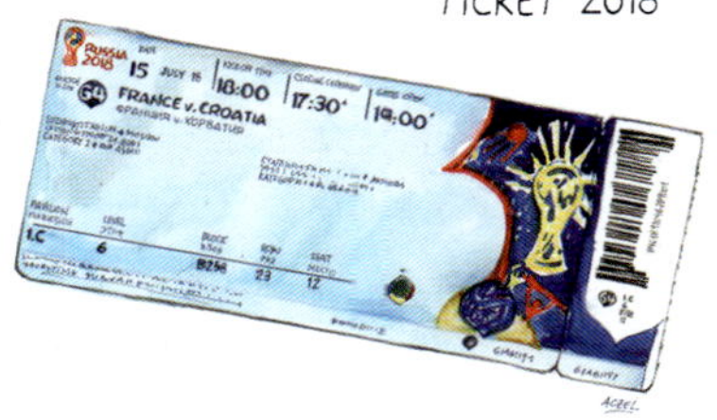

QUALIFIED TEAMS
32 (FROM 211 MEMBERS)

PLAYERS IN FIELD
590

FASTEST GOAL
55 SECONDS: ZANKA (DENMARK-CROATIA)

TOP SCORERS
GOLDEN BOOT, 6 GOALS
HARRY KANE (ENGLAND)
SILVER BOOT, 4 GOALS
ANTOINE GRIEZMANN (FRANCE)
BRONZE BOOT, 4 GOALS
ROMELU LUKAKU (BELGIUM)

BEST GOALKEEPER
THIBAUT COURTOIS (BELGIUM)

BEST YOUNG PLAYER
KYLIAN MBAPPÉ, 19 YEARS (FRANCE)

PERIOD
14TH JUNE, 2018–15TH JULY, 2018

MATCHES
64

MOST MAN OF THE MATCH
GRIEZMANN, KANE, MODRIĆ: 3

FAIR PLAY AWARD
SPAIN

YELLOW CARDS
219 (Ø: 3.42 PER MATCH)

YELLOW-RED CARDS
2 (Ø: 0.03 PER MATCH)

RED CARDS
2 (Ø: 0.03 PER MATCH)

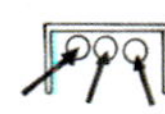

3 OR MORE GOALS IN A MATCH
3 GOALS: CRISTIANO RONALDO (PORTUGAL-SPAIN), HARRY KANE (ENGLAND-PANAMA)

ATTENDANCE
3,031,768 (Ø: 47,371 PER MATCH)

GOALS
169 (Ø: 2.64 PER MATCH)

OWN GOALS
12

MOST DANGEROUS TEAM
BELGIUM. 16 GOALS IN 7 MATCHES

BEST PLAYER
GOLDEN BALL
LUKA MODRIĆ (CROATIA)
SILVER BALL
EDEN HAZARD (BELGIUM)
BRONZE BALL
ANTOINE GRIEZMANN (FRANCE)

PENALTIES
29: 22 SCORED, 7 MISSED

DREAM TEAM 2018

ACZEL

2022 QATAR

ALL YOURS, LEO! HE COULD FINALLY KISS THE CUP. SOCCER GAVE HIM THE PRIZE HE HAD ALWAYS DESERVED. THE BEST IN THE WORLD BECAME THE WORLD CHAMPION.

2022 QATAR

A spectacular World Cup! The best World Cup ever! This was previously promised to us by the FIFA President Infantino. Probably because never before had a World Cup been so heavily criticized in advance, due to several controversies, such as the corruption involved in establishing Qatar as the host country. This edition of the event took place from November 20 to December 18. A story written in the stars: Lionel Messi, one of the best players in the history of soccer, led Argentina to glory in an epic final.

Let's start by saying that the World Cup was very well organized and ran smoothly. However, in terms of soccer, Qatar was eliminated after three losses, achieving the worst result for a host to date. The surprise team was Morocco, which became the first African team to reach the semifinals. It was the edition with the most goals ever scored: 172 (2.69 per match).

There were heartbroken stars like Neymar, CR7 and Kane, who failed to meet their own expectations. Then there was the German team, who had it in their heads to make a political statement and forgot to play soccer. A disgraceful performance: Germany did not even make it past the group stage.

Finally, there was Argentina. Not just the team, but the whole country. Lionel Messi, a global idol, finally became an indissoluble part of the Argentine national feeling and raised the third World Cup for Argentina after 36 years. The chant, "Guys, now we're excited again," created by Argentine fans to encourage his team, lent an even more emotional tone to the story.

It all started with a small slip in the first match against Saudi Arabia, reached its fiery peak in the quarterfinals against the Netherlands and ended in a final against France that could have been the plot of a Hollywood movie. The incredible 3-3 draw with the defending champions is widely regarded as the most thrilling final ever. A carousel of emotions back and forth, not suitable for the fainthearted: double French comebacks, a save by Dibu Martínez's foot in the last minute of overtime and Argentina's eternal glory in penalties.

Messi said, "I knew God would grant it to me." To be able to enjoy, one must first know how to suffer. That's it! Argentina's jersey is now decorated with the long-awaited third star, and the mission and Messi's dream have been fulfilled. No soccerer in history had maintained such a high level for so long. His nearly two-decade reign was crowned by a supreme achievement in the final stages of his career. Or will he play for the last time in 2026? He has earned the right to enjoy playing as a world champion; let him savor it.

HANDS BEHIND HIS EARS, LEGS SPREAD WIDE AND, FOR MESSI, UNUSUALLY PROVOCATIVE. THAT WAS HOW HE CELEBRATED HIS GOAL RIGHT IN FRONT OF THE DUTCH BENCH. WITH MESSI PLAYING THE BEST WORLD CUP OF HIS LIFE, NO RIVAL TACTICS COULD STOP HIM.

WELL THEN, LET'S DIVE INTO THE WORLD CUP OF THE DESERT! FOR THE FIRST TIME IN HISTORY, THE WORLD CUP WAS HELD IN AN ARAB COUNTRY—QATAR—AND FOR THE FIRST TIME IN WINTER, AS IT WOULD PROBABLY HAVE BEEN TOO HOT IN SUMMER, WITH TEMPERATURES SOARING TO 50 DEGREES EVEN IN THE SHADE. THERE ARE BEAUTIFUL, IDYLLIC IMAGES OF DESERTS, SHEIKHS, CAMELS AND FUTURISTIC STADIUMS.

SOME NEWS THAT FIFA ANNOUNCED: SEMIAUTOMATED TECHNOLOGY FOR OFFSIDE DETECTION AND A LOT OF EXTRA TIME

ACZEL

SALEM AL DAWSARI (SAUDI ARABIA) CELEBRATED THE VICTORY GOAL AGAINST ARGENTINA WITH A JUMP. IT WAS THE FIRST MATCH OF THE GROUP STAGE AND A SURPRISE DEFEAT FOR THE WHITE-AND-BLUE TEAM, WHO WERE ON A 36-GAME UNBEATEN RUN.

IN THE SECOND MATCH AGAINST MEXICO, ARGENTINA HAD TO WIN. MESSI APPEARED, PUTTING THE TEAM BACK ON THE ROAD TO SUCCESS.

RICHARLISON'S (BRAZIL) SCISSOR-KICK GOAL AGAINST SERBIA WAS VOTED THE BEST OF THE WORLD CUP

THE PLAY THAT GAVE JAPAN VICTORY OVER SPAIN: THE BALL DID NOT GO OUT AND JAPAN SCORED THE WINNER, QUALIFYING FIRST FOR THE ROUND OF 16 AND LEAVING GERMANY OUT

PLAYERS FROM GERMANY POSED WITH THEIR MOUTHS COVERED DUE TO FIFA CENSORSHIP OF THE RAINBOW ARMBAND (ONE LOVE) IN QATAR. REVENGE: QATAR TV MOCKED GERMANY AFTER THEIR EARLY ELIMINATION, MIMICKING THEIR PROTEST GESTURE.

HARRY KANE'S MISSED PENALTY AGAINST FRANCE THAT COULD HAVE CHANGED ENGLAND'S FATE: HE HAD A CHANCE TO DRAW NEAR THE END, BUT SENT HIS SHOT INTO THE CLOUDS.

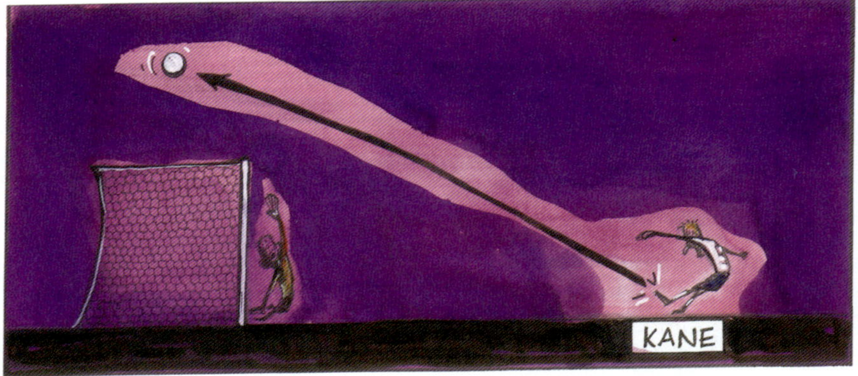

MOROCCO BEAT PORTUGAL AND MADE HISTORY AS THE FIRST AFRICAN TEAM TO REACH THE SEMIFINALS. YOUSSEF EN-NESYRI SUSPENDED HIMSELF IN MIDAIR TO HEAD HOME THE WINNING GOAL.

BY A HAIR'S BREADTH: PORTUGAL'S STAR CELEBRATED HIS TEAM'S FIRST GOAL AGAINST URUGUAY WITH HEART AND SOUL, BUT... WAS IT A GLANCING HEADER? NO, CR7 FAILED TO TOUCH THE BALL. REACHING THE RECORD OF EUSEBIO AS THE TOP PORTUGUESE GOAL SCORER IN THE WORLD CHAMPIONSHIPS NARROWLY ESCAPED HIM. TO MAKE MATTERS WORSE, FROM THE ROUND OF 16 ONWARD, CRISTIANO RONALDO WAS ELEGATED TO THE SUBSTITUTES' BENCH.

THE SOUND OF THE BALL HITTING THE POST WOULD MARK MARQUINHOS FOR LIFE. HE MISSED THE PENALTY THAT SENT BRAZIL OUT AND CERTIFIED CROATIA'S QUALIFICATION INTO THE SEMIFINALS.

WORLD CUP Qatar 2022
ACZEL

2022 WORLD CHAMPIONS: ARGENTINA.
TOP: CRISTIAN ROMERO, EMILIANO MARTÍNEZ, NICOLÁS OTAMEND , ALEXIS MAC ALLISTER, NAHUEL MOLINA. BOTTON: LIONEL MESSI, ÁNGEL DI MARÍA, RODRIGO DE PAUL, JULIÁN ALVAREZ, NICOLÁS TAGLIAFICO, ENZO FERNÁNDEZ.

THE HOTTEST MATCH

ACZEL

ARGENTINA VS. THE NETHERLANDS: THE WORLD CUP MATCH THAT SAW THE HIGHEST NUMBER OF DISCIPLINARY ACTIONS. UNFORGETTABLE: PAREDES'S HIT TOWARD THE DUTCH BENCH AND ARGENTINA'S CONTROVERSIAL CELEBRATION.

THE MOST MARADONIAN MESSI OF ALL THE WORLD CUPS. DURING AN INTERVIEW, HE PUT WEGHORST (NETHERLANDS) IN HIS PLACE, AS THE DUTCH PLAYER WAS STARING HIM DOWN AFTER BEING ELIMINATED.

A GEM FROM MESSI: THE "10" DELIVERED A MOMENT OF PURE BRILLIANCE AND TOOK GVARDIOL FOR A RIDE! ARGENTINA WAS IN THE FINAL!

THE BALL USED IN FINAL

THE FINAL 18TH DECEMBER, 2022

ARGENTINA 3:3 FRANCE

PENALTY SHOOT-OUT 4:2

LUSAIL ICONIC STADIUM, LUSAIL, QATAR
ATTENDANCE: 88,966
REFEREE: SZYMON MARCINIAK (POLAND)

LIONEL SCALONI, COACH OF THE ARGENTINE NATIONAL TEAM, LED THE "LA SCALONETA" TEAM TO WIN THE COPA AMERICA IN 2021 AND 2024, THE FINALISSIMA IN 2022 AND THE WORLD CUP IN 2022

THE BEST FINAL IN HISTORY

DEMBELE TOUCHES DI MARIA. PENALTY!

1:0

23RD MINUT

MESSI USES HIS LEFT FOOT AND HIS MASTERY TO SOFTLY EXECUTE THE PENALTY KICK

2:0

DI MARIA FINISHES AFTER A SPECTACULAR COUNTER

MBAPPÉ SCORES THE FIRST FOR FRANCE

80TH MINUTE

2:1

A FEW SECONDS LATER...

81ST MINUTE

2:2

ACZEL

...MBAPPÉ STRIKES WITH PERFECT TECHNIQUE. A SUPERB VOLLEY! WHAT A GOAL! A THRILLER AT ITS BEST!

3:2 EXTRA TIME

109TH MINUTE

MESSI TAKES ADVANTAGE OF A REBOUND

MONTIEL'S HAND. PENALTY!

118TH MINUTE

3:3 MBAPPÉ HAT TRICK

LAUTARO LOSES IT INSTANTLY. CRAZY!

...DIBU, HERO! THE FOOT OF GOD!

PENALTY SHOOT-OUT

SPECIALIST: "DIBU" MARTÍNEZ SAVES COMAN'S PENALTY KICK!

MARTÍNEZ THROWS THE BALL ON PURPOSE AS TCHOUAMÉNI MOVES TOWARD THE SPOT. THE MIND GAMES WORK...

...AND TCHOUAMÉNI THROWS IT OUT!

"DIBU" MARTÍNEZ DANCE

PENALTY SHOOT-OUT

0:1 MBAPPÉ
1:1 MESSI
MARTINEZ SAVES COMAN'S PENALTY
2:1 DYBALA
TCHOUAMÉNI THROWS IT OUT
3:1 PAREDES
3:2 KOLO MUANI
4:2 MONTIEL

WE HAVE THE THIRD ONE!
MONTIEL SCORES THE FOURTH PENALTY
AND THE DREAM BECOMES THE MOST BEAUTIFUL TRUTH.
LEO KNEELS DOWN AND PAREDES RUNS TO HUG HIM.
SOON, MORE PLAYERS JOIN IN. AT THE CENTER OF
THE CELEBRATION IS MESSI.

DIBU MARTÍNEZ'S GESTURE:
AFTER BEING AWARDED
THE "GOLDEN GLOVE,"
HE PUT THE TROPHY IN
HIS GROIN AREA. AN IMAGE
TO REMEMBER.

THE WINNERS
BEST YOUNG PLAYER:
ENZO FERNÁNDEZ
(ARGENTINA)
BEST PLAYER: LIONEL
MESSI (ARGENTINA)
BEST GOALKEEPER:
EMILIANO MARTÍNEZ
(ARGENTINA)
TOP SCORER: KYLIAN
MBAPPÉ (FRANCE)

ON THE PODIUM, THE
EMIR OF QATAR AND
FIFA PRESIDENT GIANNI
INFANTINO DRESSED
MESSI WITH A BESHT,
A TRADITIONAL
ARABIAN ROBE.
THEN CAME THE CUP.

ARGENTINA WORLD CHAMPION!

WORLD CUP @ Qat_ar2022

THAT'S IT!
THE DREAM HAS COME TRUE.

LEO WAKES UP WITH THE CUP AND TAKES HIS FIRST SIP OF MATE AS WORLD CHAMPION

FIVE MILLION ARGENTINIANS TOOK TO THE STREETS IN A MILESTONE WELCOMING CEREMONY, WITH JOY AND EMOTION LIKE NEVER SEEN BEFORE.

2022 IN OVERVIEW

GROUP A

DATE	TEAM	R	TEAM
20.11.	QATAR	0:2	ECUADOR
21.11.	SENEGAL	0:2	NETHERLANDS
25.11.	QATAR	1:3	SENEGAL
25.11.	NETHERLANDS	1:1	ECUADOR
29.11.	NETHERLANDS	2:0	QATAR
29.11.	ECUADOR	1:2	SENEGAL

PTS: NETHERLANDS 7, SENEGAL 6, ECUADOR 4, QATAR 0

GROUP B

DATE	TEAM	R	TEAM
21.11.	ENGLAND	6:2	IRAN
21.11.	USA	1:1	WALES
25.11.	WALES	0:2	IRAN
25.11.	ENGLAND	0:0	USA
29.11.	WALES	0:3	ENGLAND
29.11.	IRAN	0:1	USA

PTS: ENGLAND 7, USA 5, IRAN 3, WALES 1

GROUP C

DATE	TEAM	R	TEAM
22.11.	ARGENTINA	1:2	SAUDI ARABIA
22.11.	MEXICO	0:0	POLAND
26.11.	POLAND	2:0	SAUDI ARABIA
26.11.	ARGENTINA	2:0	MEXICO
30.11.	POLAND	0:2	ARGENTINA
30.11.	SAUDI ARABIA	1:2	MEXICO

PTS: ARGENTINA 6, POLAND 4, MEXICO 4, SAUDI ARABIA 3

GROUP D

DATE	TEAM	R	TEAM
22.11.	DENMARK	0:0	TUNISIA
22.11.	FRANCE	4:1	AUSTRALIA
26.11.	TUNISIA	0:1	AUSTRALIA
26.11.	FRANCE	2:1	DENMARK
30.11.	TUNISIA	1:0	FRANCE
30.11.	AUSTRALIA	1:0	DENMARK

PTS: FRANCE 6, AUSTRALIA 6, TUNISIA 4, DENMARK 1

GROUP E

DATE	TEAM	R	TEAM
23.11.	GERMANY	1:2	JAPAN
23.11.	SPAIN	7:0	COSTA RICA
27.11.	JAPAN	0:1	COSTA RICA
27.11.	SPAIN	1:1	GERMANY
01.12.	JAPAN	2:1	SPAIN
01.12.	COSTA RICA	2:4	GERMANY

PTS: JAPAN 6, SPAIN 4, GERMANY 4, COSTA RICA 3

GROUP F

DATE	TEAM	R	TEAM
23.11.	MOROCCO	0:0	CROATIA
23.11.	BELGIUM	1:0	CANADA
27.11.	BELGIUM	0:2	MOROCCO
27.11.	CROATIA	4:1	CANADA
01.12.	CROATIA	0:0	BELGIUM
01.12.	CANADA	1:2	MOROCCO

PTS: MOROCCO 7, CROATIA 5, BELGIUM 4, CANADA 0

GROUP G

DATE	TEAM	R	TEAM
24.11.	SWITZERLAND	1:0	CAMEROON
24.11.	BRAZIL	2:0	SERBIA
28.11.	CAMEROON	3:3	SERBIA
28.11.	BRAZIL	1:0	SWITZERLAND
02.12.	CAMEROON	1:0	BRAZIL
02.12.	SERBIA	2:3	SWITZERLAND

PTS: BRAZIL 6, SWITZERLAND 6, CAMEROON 4, SERBIA 1

GROUP H

DATE	TEAM	R	TEAM
24.11.	URUGUAY	0:0	SOUTH KOREA
24.11.	PORTUGAL	3:2	GHANA
28.11.	SOUTH KOREA	2:3	GHANA
28.11.	PORTUGAL	2:0	URUGUAY
02.12.	SOUTH KOREA	2:1	PORTUGAL
02.12.	GHANA	0:2	URUGUAY

PTS: PORTUGAL 6, SOUTH KOREA 4, URUGUAY 4, GHANA 3

ROUND OF 16

DATE	TEAM	R	TEAM
03.12.	NETHERLANDS	3:1	USA
03.12.	ARGENTINA	2:1	AUSTRALIA
04.12.	FRANCE	3:1	POLAND
04.12.	ENGLAND	3:0	SENEGAL
05.12.	JAPAN	1:1 E.T., 1:3 P.	CROATIA
05.12.	BRAZIL	4:1	SOUTH KOREA
06.12.	MOROCCO	0:0 E.T., 3:0 P.	SPAIN
06.12.	PORTUGAL	6:1	SWITZERLAND

QUARTER-FINALS

DATE	TEAM	R	TEAM
09.12.	CROATIA	1:1 E.T., 4:2 P.	BRAZIL
09.12.	NETHERLANDS	2:2 E.T., 3:4 P.	ARGENTINA
10.12.	MOROCCO	1:0	PORTUGAL
10.12.	ENGLAND	1:2	FRANCE

SEMIFINALS

DATE	TEAM	R	TEAM
13.12.	ARGENTINA	3:0	CROATIA
14.12.	FRANCE	2:0	MOROCCO

3RD PLACE

DATE	TEAM	R	TEAM
17.12.	CROATIA	2:1	MOROCCO

FINAL

DATE	TEAM	R	TEAM
18.12.	ARGENTINA	3:3 E.T., 4:2 P.	FRANCE

CHAMPION: ARGENTINA

TICKET 2022

QUALIFIED TEAMS
32 (FROM 209 MEMBERS)

PLAYERS IN FIELD
584

FASTEST GOAL

68 SECONDS: DAVIES (CANADA–CROATIA)

TOP SCORERS
GOLDEN BOOT, 8 GOALS
KYLIAN MBAPPÉ (FRANCE)
SILVER BOOT, 7 GOALS
LIONEL MESSI (ARGENTINA)
BRONZE BOOT, 4 GOALS
OLIVER GIROUD (FRANCE)

BEST GOALKEEPER
EMILIANO MARTÍNEZ (ARGENTINA)

BEST YOUNG PLAYER
ENZO FERNÁNDEZ,
21 YEARS (ARGENTINA)

PERIOD
20TH NOVEMBER, 2022–18TH DECEMBER, 2022

MATCHES
64

MOST MAN OF THE MATCH
LIONEL MESSI (ARGENTINA):
5

FAIR PLAY AWARD
ENGLAND

YELLOW CARDS
224 (Ø: 3.5 PER MATCH)

YELLOW-RED CARDS
3 (Ø: 0.05 PER MATCH)

RED CARDS
2 (Ø: 0.03 PER MATCH)

3 OR MORE GOALS IN A MATCH
3 GOALS: KYLIAN MBAPPÉ (ARGENTINA-FRANCE),
GONÇALO RAMOS (PORTUGAL-SWITZERLAND)

ATTENDANCE
3,404,252 (Ø: 53.191 PER MATCH)

GOALS
172 (Ø: 2.69 PER MATCH)

OWN GOALS
2

MOST DANGEROUS TEAM
FRANCE: 16 GOALS
IN 7 MATCHES

BEST PLAYER
GOLDEN BALL
LIONEL MESSI (ARGENTINA)
SILVER BALL
KYLIAN MBAPPÉ (FRANCE)
BRONZE BALL
LUKA MODRIĆ (CROATIA)

PENALTIES
22: 17 SCORED,
5 MISSED

DREAM TEAM 2022

SOCCER UNITES THE NATIONS

2026 USA CANADA MEXICO

A new era of the World Cup begins!
For the first time in history, a World Cup will be played in three countries: the United States, Mexico and Canada. There will be 16 cities, more than 40 stadiums and a true soccer festival across an entire continent. The biggest World Cup of all time is coming, with 48 teams and 104 matches—a gigantic tournament. FIFA promises a soccer festival with more opportunities for surprises, more excitement... but with it also comes the risk of the group stage losing some of its intensity.

The start will be special: Mexico City's Estadio Azteca—the site of Pelé's third title in 1970 and Maradona's "Hand of God" in 1986—will reopens its doors. For the third time, the opening match of a World Cup will be played there; no other stadium in the world has ever had this honor. And at the end of the tournament, all eyes will be on MetLife Stadium in New Jersey, just a stone's throw from New York, where the final will be played in front of more than 80,000 fans celebrating the new champion.

Big names will once again be in the spotlight: Lionel Messi, champion of 2022 and legend of Argentina, will hope to extend his legacy and write another historic page. Kylian Mbappé, hero of 2018 and of the last final, will continue to pursue immortality. Erling Haaland will aim to bring Norway back to the big stage after 1998. Brazil will count on Vinícius Júnior, and Germany, after the failures of 2018 and 2022, will rely on youngsters like Jamal Musiala and Florian Wirtz to bring fresh energy.

Cristiano Ronaldo will also be on the scene, probably playing in his last World Cup, just like Messi.

Outsiders will be waiting for their opportunity: Morocco, a semifinalist in 2022, will hope to prove that its success was no accident. The United States will dream of becoming bigger at home. Mexico and Canada will look to surprise in front of their home crowd. And, perhaps, another unexpected team will achieve what Croatia, Iceland, Uruguay or Cameroon once did: win the hearts of the fans. One thing is certain: 2026 will not just be a World Cup, but an XXL global event. A tournament full of promises, questions and new stories, with Messi and Argentina as central protagonists, ready to defend their title. Who will be crowned in the end?

WORLD CUP STARS 2026

WHEN THE WORLD CUP BECOMES THE STAGE OF DREAMS

LIONEL MESSI (ARGENTINA)

KYLIAN MBAPPÉ (FRANCE)

ACHRAF HAKIMI (MOROCCO)

THOMAS PARTEY (GHANA)

AJDIN HRUSTIC (AUSTRALIA)

GIANLUIGI DONNARUMMA (ITALY)

NEYMAR JR. (BRAZIL)

ERLING HAALAND (NORWAY)

KEYLOR NAVAS (COSTA RICA)

ALPHONSO DAVIES (CANADA)

CHRISTIAN PULISIC (USA)

HIRVING LOZANO (MEXICO)

MEHDI TAREMI (IRAN)

MEMPHIS DEPAY (NETHERLANDS)

HARRY KANE (ENGLAND)

YANN SOMMER (SWITZERLAND)

LAMINE YAMAL (SPAIN)

KEVIN DE BRUYNE (BELGIUM)

KARL TOKO EKAMBI (CAMEROON)

ALI MAALOUL (TUNISIA)

CHRISTIAN ERIKSEN (DENMARK)

KAORU MITOMA (JAPAN)

ROBERT LEWANDOWSKI (POLAND)

CRISTIANO RONALDO (PORTUGAL)

LUCA MODRIĆ (CROATIA)

ENNER VALENCIA (ECUADOR)

MOHAMED SALAH (EGYPT)

SON HEUNG-MIN (SOUTH KOREA)

MANUEL NEUER (GERMANY)

2026

11TH JUNE – 19TH JULY 2026

48 TEAMS

104 MATCHES

2026 WORLD CUP

UNITED STATES CANADA MÉXICO

GROUP A

PLACE	DATE/MATCH		TEAM	
1.	11.06.	1	MEXICO	SOUTH AFRICA
3.	11.06.	2	SOUTH KOREA	A4
13.	18.06.	25	A4	SOUTH AFRICA
3.	18.06.	28	MEXICO	SOUTH KOREA
1.	24.06.	53	A4	MEXICO
2.	24.06.	54	SOUTH AFRICA	SOUTH KOREA

*

GROUP E

PLACE	DATE/MATCH		TEAM	
11.	14.06.	10	GERMANY	CURAÇAO
9.	14.06.	9	IVORY COAST	ECUADOR
14.	20.06.	33	GERMANY	IVORY COAST
10.	20.06.	34	ECUADOR	CURAÇAO
7.	25.06.	56	ECUADOR	GERMANY
9.	25.06.	55	CURAÇAO	IVORY COAST

GROUP B

PLACE	DATE/MATCH		TEAM	
14.	12.06.	3	CANADA	B2
5.	13.06.	8	QATAR	SWITZERLAND
4.	18.06.	26	SWITZERLAND	B2
15.	18.06.	27	CANADA	QATAR
15.	24.06.	51	SWITZERLAND	CANADA
6.	24.06.	52	B2	QATAR

*

GROUP F

PLACE	DATE/MATCH		TEAM	
12.	14.06.	11	NETHERLANDS	JAPAN
2.	14.06.	12	F3	TUNISIA
11.	20.06.	35	NETHERLANDS	F3
2.	20.06.	36	TUNISIA	JAPAN
10.	25.06.	58	TUNISIA	NETHERLANDS
12.	25.06.	57	JAPAN	F3

*

GROUP C

PLACE	DATE/MATCH		TEAM	
7.	13.06.	7	BRAZIL	MOROCCO
8.	13.06.	5	HAITI	SCOTLAND
9.	19.06.	29	BRAZIL	HAITI
8.	19.06.	30	SCOTLAND	MOROCCO
16.	24.06.	49	SCOTLAND	BRAZIL
13.	24.06.	50	MOROCCO	HAITI

GROUP G

PLACE	DATE/MATCH		TEAM	
6.	15.06.	16	BELGIUM	EGYPT
4.	15.06.	15	IRAN	NEW ZEALAND
4.	21.06.	39	BELGIUM	IRAN
15.	21.06.	40	NEW ZEALAND	EGYPT
15.	26.06.	64	NEW ZEALAND	BELGIUM
6.	26.06.	63	EGYPT	IRAN

GROUP D

PLACE	DATE/MATCH		TEAM	
4.	12.06.	4	USA	PARAGUAY
15.	13.06.	6	AUSTRALIA	D4
5.	19.06.	31	D4	PARAGUAY
6.	19.06.	32	USA	AUSTRALIA
4.	25.06.	59	D4	USA
5.	25.06.	60	PARAGUAY	AUSTRALIA

GROUP H

PLACE	DATE/MATCH		TEAM	
13.	15.06.	14	SPAIN	CAPE VERDE
16.	15.06.	13	SAUDI ARABIA	URUGUAY
13.	21.06.	38	SPAIN	SAUDI ARABIA
16.	21.06.	37	URUGUAY	CAPE VERDE
3.	26.06.	66	URUGUAY	SPAIN
11.	26.06.	65	CAPE VERDE	SAUDI ARABIA

* A4: UEFA PATH D WINNER, D4: UEFA PATH C WINNER, F3: UEFA PATH B WINNER, I3: IC PATH 2 WINNER, K2: IC PATH 1 WINNER

GROUP I

PLACE	DATE/MATCH		TEAM	
7.	16.06.	17	FRANCE	SENEGAL
8.	16.06.	18	i3	NORWAY
9.	22.06.	42	FRANCE	i3
7.	22.06.	41	NORWAY	SENEGAL
8.	26.06.	61	NORWAY	FRANCE
14.	26.06.	62	SENEGAL	i3

*

GROUP J

PLACE	DATE/MATCH		TEAM	
10.	16.06.	19	ARGENTINA	ALGERIA
5.	16.06.	20	AUSTRIA	JORDAN
12.	22.06.	43	ARGENTINA	AUSTRIA
5.	22.06.	44	JORDAN	ALGERIA
12.	27.06	70	JORDAN	ARGENTINA
10.	27.06	69	ALGERIA	AUSTRIA

GROUP K

PLACE	DATE/MATCH		TEAM	
11.	17.06.	23	PORTUGAL	K2
1.	17.06.	24	UZBEKISTAN	COLOMBIA
11.	23.06.	47	PORTUGAL	UZBEKISTAN
3.	23.06.	48	COLOMBIA	K2
16.	27.06.	71	COLOMBIA	PORTUGAL
13.	27.06.	72	K2	UZBEKISTAN

*

GROUP L

PLACE	DATE/MATCH		TEAM	
12.	17.06.	22	ENGLAND	CROATIA
14.	17.06.	21	GHANA	PANAMA
8.	23.06.	45	ENGLAND	GHANA
14.	23.06.	46	PANAMA	CROATIA
7.	27.06	67	PANAMA	ENGLAND
9.	27.06	68	CROATIA	GHANA

ROUND OF 32

PLACE	DATE/MATCH		TEAM	
8.	29.06.	74	E1	ABCDF3
7.	30.06.	77	i1	CDFGH3
4.	28.06.	73	A2	B2
2.	29.06.	75	F1	C2
14.	02.07.	83	K2	L2
4.	02.07.	84	H1	J2

5.	01.07.	81	D1	BEFIJ3
6.	01.07.	82	G1	AEHIJ3
11.	29.06.	76	C1	F2
12.	30.06.	78	E2	i2
1.	30.06.	79	A1	CEFHi3
13.	01.07.	80	L1	EHiJK3

16.	03.07.	86	J1	H2
12.	03.07.	88	D2	G2
15.	02.07.	85	B1	EFGiJ3
10.	03.07.	87	K1	DEiJL3

PLACES:

1. AZTECA STADIUM, MEXICO CITY
2. MONTERREY STADIUM
3. GUADALAJARA STADIUM
4. LOS ANGELES STADIUM
5. SAN FRANCISCO BAY AREA STADIUM
6. SEATTLE STADIUM
7. NEW YORK/NEW JERSEY STADIUM
8. BOSTON STADIUM
9. PHILADELPHIA STADIUM
10. KANSAS CITY STADIUM
11. HOUSTON STADIUM
12. DALLAS STADIUM
13. ATLANTA STADIUM
14. TORONTO STADIUM
15. BC PLACE VANCOUVER
16. MIAMI STADIUM

ACZEL

2026 WORLD CUP

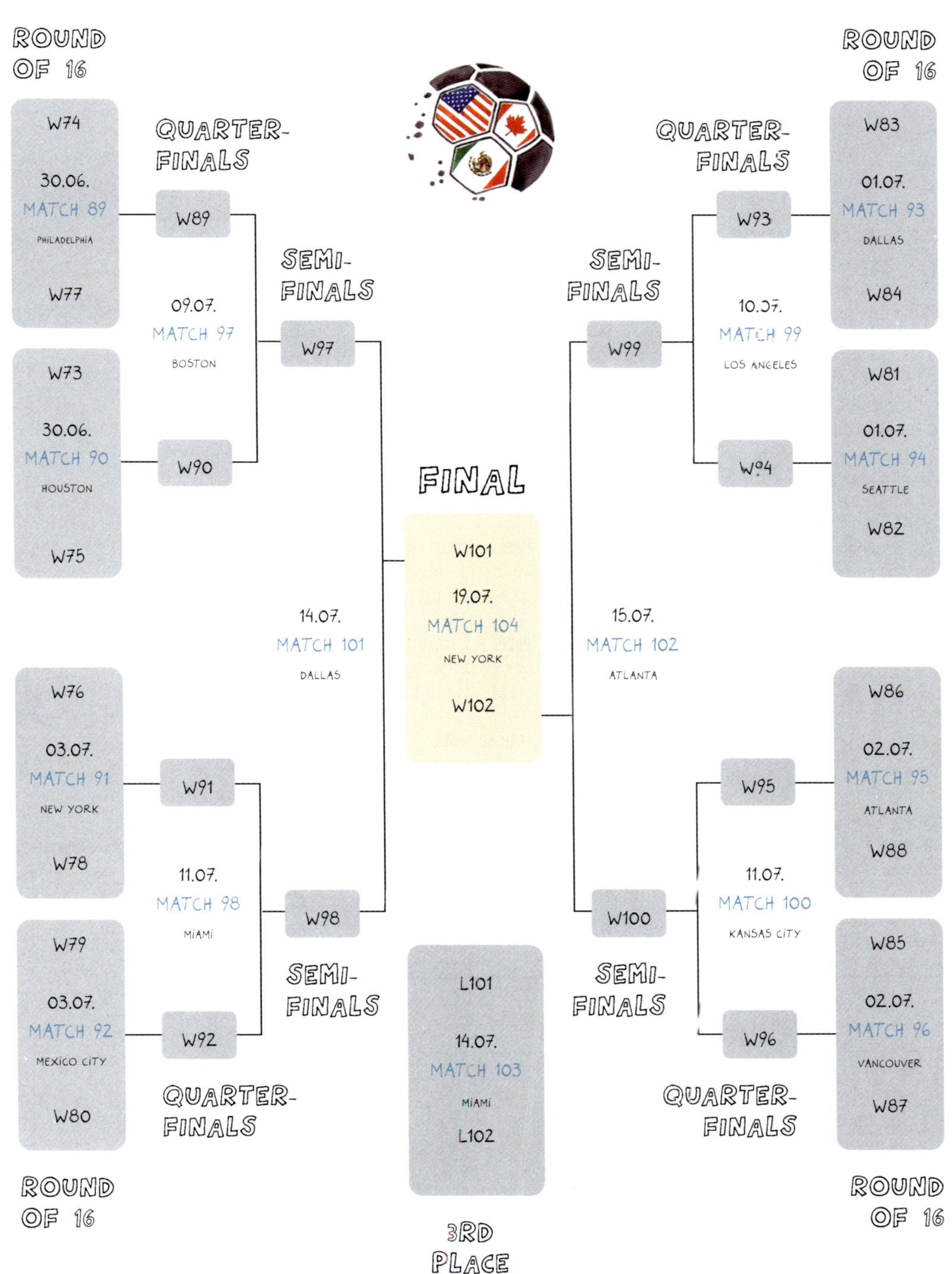

ALL WORLD CUPS IN OVERVIEW

CHAMPIONSHIPS
BRAZIL: 5
GERMANY: 4
ITALY: 4
ARGENTINA: 3
URUGUAY: 2
FRANCE: 2
ENGLAND, SPAIN: 1

MOST FINAL PARTICIPATIONS
GERMANY: 8
BRAZIL: 7
ITALY: 6
ARGENTINA: 6
NETHERLANDS, FRANCE: 3

TOP SCORERS
MIROSLAV KLOSE: 16
RONALDO: 15
GERD MÜLLER: 14
JUST FONTAINE, MESSI: 13
PELÉ, MBAPPÉ: 12
JÜRGEN KLINSMANN: 11
SANDOR KOCSIS: 11

MOST MATCHES PLAYED
BRAZIL: 114
GERMANY: 112
ARGENTINA: 88
ITALY: 83
ENGLAND: 74
SPAIN: 67

BIGGEST SCORELINE
HUNGARY– EL SALVADOR
10:1 (1982)

RECORD MATCH: 2014, BRAZIL–GERMANY 1:7
- THE FASTEST FOUR GOALS SCORED (4 GOALS IN 6 MINUTES)
- FASTEST BRACE: TONI KROOS 2 GOALS IN 69 SECONDS
- WITH KHEDIRA SCORING THE 0:5, GERMANY ALSO OVERTOOK BRAZIL TO BECOME THE ALL-TIME HIGHEST-SCORING TEAM
- BIGGEST WINNING MARGIN IN A SEMIFINAL, THE WORST LOSS BY A HOST COUNTRY AND FOR BRAZIL
- HIGHEST 2014 WIN
- THE ONLY SQUAD TO REACH 8 FINALS

MIROSLAV KLOSE:
- ONLY PLAYER TO TAKE PART IN FOUR SEMIFINALS
- HE SCORED THE 0:2 AND BROKE THE RECORD OF MOST GOALS SCORED, WITH 16 GOALS, OVERTAKING BRAZIL'S RONALDO'S TOTAL OF 15

SOCIAL MEDIA AND TV:
- 35.6 MILLION TWEETS
- 32.57 MILLION TV VIEWERSHIP ONLY IN GERMANY
- 200 MILLIONS POSTS ON FACEBOOK

MESSI: MOST APPEARANCES AS CAPTAIN: 19.
HE IS THE ONLY PLAYER TO PROVIDE AN ASSIST IN FIVE WORLD CUPS.

PELÉ: YOUNGEST GOALSCORER: 17 YEARS, 1958.
YOUNGEST WORLD CHAMPION: 17 YEARS, 1958.
MOST WORLD CUP WINS: 3 (1958, 1962, 1970).

MARADONA:
GOAL OF THE CENTURY: 1986. MOST VOTES RECEIVED FOR FIFA WORLD CUP DREAM TEAM.

MOST MATCHES PLAYED

	PLAYER	TEAM	WORLD CUP	M
1.	LIONEL MESSI	ARGENTINA	2006, 2010, 2014, 2018, 2022	26
2.	LOTHAR MATTHÄUS	GERMANY	1982, 1986, 1990, 1994, 1998	25
3.	MIROSLAV KLOSE	GERMANY	2002, 2006, 2010, 2014	24
4.	PAOLO MALDINI	ITALY	1990, 1994, 1998, 2002	23
5.	DIEGO MARADONA	ARGENTINA	1982, 1986, 1990, 1994	21
	UWE SEELER	GERMANY	1958, 1962, 1966, 1970	21
	WŁADYSŁAW ŻMUDA	POLAND	1974, 1978, 1982, 1986	21
6.	CAFU	BRAZIL	1994, 1998, 2002, 2006	20
	PHILIPP LAHM	GERMANY	2006, 2010, 2014	20
	B. SCHWEINSTEIGER	GERMANY	2006, 2010, 2014	20
	GRZEGORZ LATO	POLAND	1974, 1978, 1982	20

MOST MATCHES WON IN PENALTY SHOOT-OUTS

	LAND	PSO	WON	LOST
1.	ARGENTINA	7	1990 (QF AND SF), 1998 (R16), 2014 (SF), 2022 (QF AND F)	2006 (QF)
2.	GERMANY	4	1982 (SF), 1986 (QF), 1990 (SF), 2006 (QF)	-
	CROATIA	4	2018 (R16 AND QF), 2022 (R16 AND QF)	-
3.	BRAZIL	5	1994 (F), 1998 (SF), 2014 (R16)	1986 (QF), 2022 (QF)

QUALIFIED TEAMS
79

PERIOD
13TH JULY, 1930 – 22ND DECEMBER, 2022

ATTENDANCE
40,532,478

PLAYERS IN FIELD
7,781

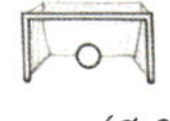

GOALS
2,720
(Ø 2.82 PER MATCH)

OWN GOALS
54
(Ø 0.06 PER MATCH)

FASTEST GOAL

2002: 11 SECONDS HAKAN ŞÜKÜR
(TURKEY–SOUTH KOREA)

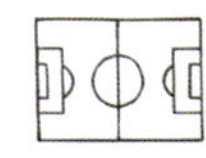

MATCHES PLAYED
964

MOST DANGEROUS TEAM
BRAZIL WITH
237 GOALS IN 114 MATCHES
(Ø 2.07 PER MATCH)

TOP SHOCK MOMENT
ZIDANE VS. MATERAZZI (2006)

YELLOW CARDS
2,303 (Ø 2.55 PER MATCH)

YELLOW/RED CARDS
47 (Ø 0.06 PER MATCH)

RED CARDS
124 (Ø 0.13 PER MATCH)

PENALTIES
227: 185 SCORED,
42 MISSED/SAVED

MOST PENALTY SHOOT-OUT LOSSES
ENGLAND, ITALY AND SPAIN (3 FROM 4)

MOST SENDING OFFS: 2: RIGOBERT SONG (CAMEROON) AND ZINEDINE ZIDANE (FRANCE)

MOST PARTICIPATIONS: 22, BRAZIL

MOST WINS (TEAM): 76, BRAZIL

MOST WINS (PLAYER): 17, MIROSLAV KLOSE (GERMANY, 2002–2014)

MOST MINUTES PLAYED: 2,314 MINUTES, LIONEL MESSI (ARGENTINA, 2006–2022)

HIGHEST AVERAGE OF GOALS SCORED: HUNGARY 1954 (27 IN 5 MATCHES; 5.4 PER MATCH)

MOST GOALS SCORED IN A TOURNAMENT: JUST FONTAINE (FRANCE, 1958, 13 GOALS IN 6 MATCHES)

MOST GOALS SCORED IN A MATCH: 5, OLEG SALENKO (RUSSIA, 1994, VS CAMEROON)

MOST MATCHES COACHED: HELMUT SCHÖN (GERMANY, 1966–1978)

OLDEST CHAMPION: DINO ZOFF, 40 YEARS (ITALY, 1982)

MOST GOALS IN A MATCH: 12 (7:5 AUSTRIA–SWITZERLAND, 1954)

FASTEST GOAL BY A SUBSTITUTE: RICHARD MORALES, 16 SECONDS (URUGUAY–SENEGAL, 2002)

DREAM TEAM OF ALL-TIME

THE AUTHOR

Germán Aczel was born on February 12, 1974 in Buenos Aires, Argentina. He spent his school days drawing. On Mondays, his teachers and classmates would eagerly wait for his illustrations of the goals of Boca Juniors. At the age of 16, he was already publishing in local media.

After winning his first awards, he began working for Argentina's leading daily newspaper, *La Nación*, and shortly thereafter for the country's most important sports journal, *El Gráfico*.

At the age of 20, he had his first major exposure and also represented Argentina at the international level. After living in Rio de Janeiro, Brazil, and working for *Jornal do Brasil*, among others, Aczel traveled to Europe at the age of 26 with the prize money he had won in a cartoonists' competition in Dubai. In Munich, he met his wife while dancing tango, and he stayed there. In Germany, he drew for *BRAVO Sport*, *Bundesliga* and the English magazine *FourFourTwo*, among others.

Aczel is the author of the book *World Cup 1930–2026*, the first version of which was published in 2010 in nine countries, including England, Italy and France. In 2014, it was published for the first time in Germany, where it became a bestseller, as well as in China in 2018. In 2022, his new book on soccer, called *The Greatest Goals of All Time*, was launched in Germany. It sold out quickly and had a great impact on the press. In 2024 and 2025, two new books appeared: *Oooh, wie ist das schön!* (2024) and *Tor für Deutschland!* (2025), both dedicated to the German national team.

His drawings are part of the FIFA Museum in Zurich, Switzerland, where one of his original drawings is also on display. The museum invited him to be their Artist in Residence during the 2018 World Cup to document the events through his drawings.

He was invited by Abu Dhabi Media to design the last page of the *Al-Ittihad* daily newspaper during the 2019 Asian Cup in UAE. In 2022, an exclusive exhibition was held in Vaduz, Liechtenstein, at the Vaduzersaal, dedicated to the best goals of the World Cups, as part of a special public viewing.

He supports UNICEF and the Homeless World Cup and promotes sports integration for refugees. The Argentine artist currently lives with his wife and four children in Munich, Germany.

DEDICATED TO MY CHILDREN AND ALL SOCCER FANS!

IMPRINT

www.germanaczel.com

Revised and Expanded New Edition: 1st Edition 2026

Idea and Illustrations: Germán Aczel
Text: Chris Fritz and Germán Aczel

English Translation: Paula Silvina Cagnoni
Cover: Germán Aczel

Layout: Germán Aczel and
Groothuis. Gesellschaft der Ideen
und Passionen mbH, Hamburg | www.groothuis.de

This edition of the book is published by Wonder House Books
An Imprint of Prakash Books

wonderhousebooks.com

wonderhousebooks/
wonderhousebook
wonderhousebooks

Printed in China.
ISBN 978-93-87779-25-9

Wonder House Team Credits:

Acquisition by: Payal Jaipuria, Executive Publisher

Creative Team
Manpreet Kaur, Tausif Ali Khan, Devangana Ojha, Erende Sangma, Dinesh Sharma

FIFA